P9-CDZ-457

Penguin Education

Penguin Modern Psychology
General Editor: B. M. Foss

Cognitive Psychology
Editors:
P. C. Dodwell and Anne Treisman

Psycholinguistics
Chomsky and Psychology
Judith Greene

Judith Greene

Psycholinguistics
Chomsky and Psychology

Penguin Education

Penguin Education
A Division of Penguin Books Ltd,
Harmondsworth, Middlesex, England
Penguin Books Inc, 7110 Ambassador Road,
Baltimore, Md 21207, USA
Penguin Books Australia Ltd,
Ringwood, Victoria, Australia
Penguin Books Canada Ltd,
41 Steelcase Road West,
Markham, Ontario, Canada

First published 1972
Reprinted 1973, 1974
Copyright © Judith Greene 1972

Made and printed in Great Britain by
Richard Clay (The Chaucer Press) Ltd, Bungay, Suffolk
Set in Monotype Times New Roman

To Graham

Contents

Part Two
Psychological Experiments

Editorial Foreword

It is often claimed that language is what most distinguishes man from other animals. What then is language? In 1957 two books were published epitomizing two extreme positions: Skinner's *Verbal Behavior* was a most elaborate culmination of a traditional, stimulus-response, learning theory approach, while Chomsky's *Syntactic Structures* launched a new linguistic theory known as transformational grammar, which has since revolutionized psycholinguists' aims and ideas about language.

Dr Greene's book is one of the clearest and most readable accounts of this revolution, of the theory which started it, and of the continuing progress and interaction of linguistics and psychological research. The relation between the two subjects poses fascinating but very difficult problems which have been clarified but not yet solved. For example, while the linguist's grammar tries to specify the nature of the language which is expressed or responded to in the behaviour studied by the psychologist, the validity of this grammar itself depends on psychological data in the form of spoken utterances and the intuitions humans have about their structure. These intuitions can vary widely, from the judgement in 1957 that 'colourless green ideas sleep furiously' is grammatical, to the judgement in 1971 that 'even John came, but then maybe no-one else did' is *un*grammatical; this variation has implications which linguists have perhaps not fully acknowledged.

On the psychological side, Dr Greene has chosen to concentrate on the more important studies of adults' understanding, recall and production of language, testing weak and strong claims of the psychological reality of Chomsky's grammar. There is little on the child's acquisition of language or on phonology and speech. She mentions briefly the most recent linguistic developments, Fillmore's case grammar and the generative semantics approach, but feels these have not yet been proved incompatible with Chomsky's account, which provoked all the psychological experiments reviewed here. Of these she makes a lucid, reasoned and well-structured survey, fascinating both in the ideas discussed and as a historical account of research in progress. She shows how the early, misleadingly successful experiments on syntax have been superseded by more sophisticated attempts to sort out the roles of syntax and semantics in determining performance. An original contribution is her demonstration that the wheel then comes back in a more satisfying circle via the information processing account of comprehension to Chomsky's deep structure plus transformational markers. Throughout the book she gives her own assessment of the validity and consistency of the theories, and succeeds in the difficult achievement of telling a coherent, comprehensible story without slurring over or glibly ignoring the major remaining problems.

Although this book concentrates on theoretical issues rather than their wider and more practical relevance, their importance in many other fields should be clear. The nature and treatment of language disorders, the best method of teaching native and foreign languages in schools, the possibility of machine translation and the effective use of mass-communication techniques are but a few examples of areas in which some knowledge of the nature of language and its use is essential to further progress. But such knowledge is also of fundamental importance to any growth in our understanding of the human mind.

A.T.

Preface

The psycholinguistic revolution inspired by Noam Chomsky's theory of transformational grammar is a true revolution, in the sense that its basic concepts have so shaped our way of looking at language that they are in danger of being taken for granted. Just as the Freudian outlook has permeated our attitudes to personality, so it is not always easy to make the imaginative leap back to the 'dark ages' of pre-Chomskyan investigations of verbal responses. Further evidence of the revolutionary nature of psycholinguistics is the recent emergence of a counter-revolutionary movement. Its supporters point out the many real difficulties involved in the attempt to use Chomskyan linguistics as a basis for psychological models of language, but perhaps without always realizing that these difficulties are the reverse side of the now generally accepted 'creativity' of linguistic rules. Intractable as these problems are, they cannot be got rid of by sweeping awkward linguistic insights under the carpet. It seems rather to be the case that increasing complications reflect a more accurate picture of the complexity of language behaviour.

The aim of this book is to try and bring out the reasons why transformational grammar should have interested psychologists in the first place, or in other words what all the fuss is about. It is only with an understanding of this, that the seriousness of the difficulties raised by psychological applications of the theory can be appreciated. Far from being the result of arbitrary linguistic theorising, they are at the very root of human functioning as a rule-using animal.

The 'plotting' of the book in two complementary parts (the first devoted to generative linguistic theory and the second to psychological research) will, it is hoped, illuminate interconnections between the two disciplines. It also allows the reader the option of following through the 1957 and 1965 versions of Chomsky's theory directly from theory to experiment.

A word about the choice of experiments selected for discussion in Part Two; this was guided not so much by the aim of presenting a compendium of experimental references, but rather with the idea of taking up in some detail lines of research which highlight the principles and problems of psycholinguistics. As a result, while some topics have been covered at some length, due to inevitable lack of space other areas have been left virtually untouched, notably phonetics and phonology and language acquisition. Important as these undoubtedly are, adequate coverage would require another book at least as long as the present one.

Finally, I would like to thank Frances Bundock and Elizabeth Robinson, without whose help in organizing the typing this book would have remained far longer a manuscript scrawl.

Introduction: Why Psycholinguistics?

What justification is there – apart from fashion – for using the newly coined 'psycholinguistics' in place of the perfectly serviceable 'psychology of language'? I shall argue that the new term represents a real shift from earlier approaches to language behaviour, indicating as it does a confrontation between the two disciplines of linguistics and psychology. Before going further, however, it is important to grasp that psycholinguistics remains a sub-discipline of psychology, the distinctive feature of which is that its practitioners believe in the value of looking to linguistics for an analysis of language. The following account of the beginnings of psycholinguistics will, therefore, be solely concerned with those aspects of linguistics which have been taken up, for good or ill, by psychologists as being relevant to psychological theories of language behaviour.

In order to set the stage, a brief description of the climate of opinion just prior to the advent of psycholinguistics is in order. The two major influences on psychologists studying language were information theory and learning theory. Looking at information theory first, according to the technical definition of information introduced in Shannon's theory of telecommunications (Shannon and Weaver, 1949), what is important is not the content of a message but the probability that it will be transmitted. This means that the output of language users can be looked at as a set of message sequences in which each word has a definable probability of occurring. The implication is that it is these probabilities that control individual speakers' outputs and their ability to process language. Experiments carried out by George Miller (1951) and others showed that varying the probabilities of words and letters occurring in different contexts has a significant effect on subjects' language performance.

From the point of view of learning theory, verbal responses are thought of as a sub-class of responses in general. Consequently, they can be explained by the general laws governing the establishment of connections between stimuli and responses, although there is disagreement about how complicated the stimulus-response connections may need to be in the case of complex behaviour such as problem solving, thinking and language. The simplest account is Skinner's (1957), claiming that verbal responses are directly attached to stimuli without any need for intervening variables such as meaning, ideas or grammatical rules. Mainly associated with Osgood (Osgood, Suci and Tannenbaum, 1957) is mediation learning theory, which treats meanings as symbolic mediation processes. These are unobservable meaning responses to words, which represent only a part of the overt response that would have been made to the object, and in turn stimulate appropriate responses to the word. Osgood's theory in its original version concentrated on measurement of meaning responses to individual words, with less emphasis placed on the problem of how word meanings are combined to produce meaningful statements. As with information theory, the stimulus-response approach is concerned with the probability that a particular verbal response will occur, in this case due to a previous history of conditioning.

When the term 'psycholinguistics' first began to be used in the early 1950s, it indicated a concern with linguistic methods for describing the output of language users; in particular, structural analysis into linguistic units such as phonemes, morphemes and phrases (for definitions see page 44ff.), which appeared to offer a more precise formulation of such obviously psychological units as letters, words and sentences. But the important point about this early use of the term is that interest in linguistic analysis coexisted quite happily with information theory and learning theory approaches to describing language behaviour (see, for example, the account of a psycholinguistics research seminar first published in 1954 and reprinted in Osgood and Sebeok, 1965). The implicit underlying assumption was that experience of conditioned stimulus-response associations between linguistic units, or between linguistic units and the objects to which they refer, would determine the probability of a meaningful response; and, moreover, that it is these stimulus-response probabilities operating in the behaviour of the individual speaker that are responsible for the overall frequencies of linguistic units found in large samples of language output.

This state of tripartite co-existence between information theory, learning theory and linguistic analysis lasted until 1960, when the work of the linguist Noam Chomsky was first introduced to psychologists in Miller, Galanter and Pribram's seminal book, *Plans and the Structure of Behaviour* (1960). Certainly, one obvious question that is likely to occur to anyone exposed to psycholinguistics for the first time is: given that it is reasonable to make use of linguistic descriptions of language, why should such exclusive attention be paid to just this one linguist, Noam Chomsky? The plain answer is that Chomsky's theory of generative transformational grammar was the first to force psychologists to reconsider their whole approach to the study of language behaviour, and so heralded the psycholinguistic 'revolution'.

The major change as far as psychology is concerned is that Chomsky's linguistic theory makes explicit a definition of language which appears to rule out the possibility of linguistic analysis continuing in tandem with information theory and learning theory accounts of response probabilities and conditioned word meanings. The arguments used by Chomsky and his supporters were designed to show, first, that learning theory is in principle unable to account for the speaker's ability to use language, and second, that, in any case, acquisition of stimulus-response probabilities would be a wildly uneconomical explanation of language learning. On the first count, the crucial point is Chomsky's demonstration that the number of possible grammatical sentences is potentially infinite, since it is always possible for a speaker to produce some new combination of words not spoken before. Obviously, it is theoretically impossible to calculate the probability of words occurring together in a new combination on the basis of previous frequencies of occurrence. Chomsky's famous sentence *Colourless green ideas sleep furiously* is an example of a sequence of words which is immediately recognizable as a grammatical sentence despite the infinitesimal probability of any of the words having occurred together before. The point he is making is that there is no theoretical limit to the number of novel sentences that can be produced; consequently a speaker's performance cannot be based on probability counts of the finite sample of sentences he happens to have already experienced.

The second consideration is the implausibility of the notion that, even supposing there were some artificial limit placed on the number of possible sentences, a child could learn a language by experiencing all possible sentence strings in order to become aware of the probabilities of stimulus-response associations between successive words in a sentence. Apart from the theoretical impossibility of making this calculation, it would obviously be far more efficient for the child to develop rules for producing permissible sentence sequences, including combinations of words he has never heard before, and which consequently have no calculable probability of occurring.

In a review of Skinner's *Verbal Behaviour*, Chomsky (1959) criticized any attempt to explain the ability to produce novel sentences in terms of generalization of word classes and sentence frames. To take just one example given by Chomsky, the two following word sequences have the same sentence frame cues: *Furiously sleep ideas green colourless* and *Friendly young dogs seem harmless*, and yet only one is a grammatical sentence. Chomsky's argument is that it is difficult to see how the native speaker's awareness of this fact can be explained except by stretching the concept' of generalization of physically similar stimuli so far beyond its original sense that it becomes meaningless.

Faced with these arguments about what language behaviour is *not*, psychologists reacted in several ways. Skinner has remained unrepentant, a fact that may have something to do with the somewhat vitriolic tone of Chomsky's original review.

As will be argued in the final assessment of Chomsky's theory as a basis for psychological models, the so far unreconcilable disagreement between Skinner and Chomsky is largely due to the fact that they are looking at different aspects of language, each refusing to admit the existence of the problems being tackled by the other. Osgood, on the other hand, has taken up an intermediate position, attempting to reconcile response probabilities with the use of grammatical rules within representational mediation learning theory; a position that will be discussed in later chapters. Finally, there were the immediate converts, notably George Miller, who emphasized not only the negative arguments following from Chomsky's theory but also its positive implications for the psychology of language.

From this point of view, the importance of Chomsky's generative theory lies in its central emphasis on the 'creative' aspect of the language user's ability to produce novel sentences he has never uttered or heard before. By making it the avowed aim of transformational grammar to provide a set of rules for generating the infinite number of possible sentences in a language, Chomsky appeared to be offering an exact correlate of the rules which enable a native speaker to produce all the sentences of his language. To recreate the sense of excitement aroused by this interpretation of generative grammar, one only has to imagine the discovery of an equivalent program of formal rules to mimic other complex human processes such as problem-solving or memorization. In these areas psychologists can only look at the indirect effect of subjects' presumed rule strategies; in the case of language they can turn to Chomsky's generative linguistics for a complete account of the rule operations necessary for sentence production.

At this point, attention must be drawn to a major source of future misunderstanding. When Chomsky describes his theory as defining the linguistic competence of a native speaker, this can be taken in two ways. First, that a grammar is simply a description of overall language output, expressed in the form of linguistic rules for generating sentences that match the potential output of native speakers. The second interpretation is that the rules of transformational grammar represent the actual operations used by speakers to utter sentences. This fundamental ambiguity, enshrined as the competence/performance issue, brings into the open a problem that also applied to earlier approaches. Because word frequency analysis of a sample of speech turns up certain probabilities, does this mean that individual speakers actually calculate these probabilities when speaking? Chomsky has argued that such probability calculating operations are incapable of reproducing the potentially infinite characteristics of language revealed by generative theory. But, equally, does a demonstration that the rules of transformational grammar will generate the infinite number of possible sentences in a language constitute proof of the stronger hypothesis that these rules are actually used by speakers to produce sentences? This is a question to which we shall repeatedly return.

What is certain is that this has been a creative misunderstanding. The exciting idea that linguistic rules are themselves a prototype of the language user's behaviour has stimulated a new way of looking at language and the development of new experimental techniques for testing it. It is true that further research has tended to throw up many complicating factors, including some that have been neglected as a result of the wholesale condemnation of stimulus-response theory; but this is a healthy sign of psychologists' more realistic appreciation of the complexities of language behaviour.

One final point that is of great interest to psychologists is the question of whether the laws governing language behaviour are special to human language or are characteristic of all behaviour, as would be maintained by the stimulus-response theorists. Traditionally, linguists have studied only the 'natural' languages used by members of human communities to communicate with each other. This cuts out wider senses of communication to which some psychologists would subscribe, including both animal signal systems and human mathematical and logical codes which can be used to transmit messages. (It is because of this concern with natural language that modern linguists are primarily interested in spoken speech; when dealing with written speech they are concerned only with 'spontaneous' linguistic reactions rather than 'artificial' logical operations perhaps involving paper and pencil analysis. As we shall see, it is a disadvantage of much psychological experimentation that, for obvious practical reasons, written material is often used under conditions in which logical operations can be employed in addition to purely linguistic processes).

Chomsky in particular has taken the position that acquisition of the generative rules found in natural languages requires a distinctive linguistic capacity, thus emphasizing the differences between specifically linguistic and other cognitive abilities. In view of this, it is, perhaps, paradoxical that in the Miller, Galanter and Pribram book (1960) Chomsky's theory is presented as one example of a general re-thinking of the processes involved in human cognitive functioning. As far as psychology is concerned, then, Chomsky's demonstration of the need for rules to produce language has had an important effect on the analysis of many cognitive, perceptual and even motor skills. Reversing the claim that even such complex skills as verbal behaviour can be explained in terms of peripheral chains of stimulus-response associations, Miller, Galanter and Pribram take the opposite position that virtually all behaviour needs to be centrally planned, in the same way that a computer is programmed to carry out certain routines and sub-routines subject to a master program. It is very easy to think of these programmed instructions as rules which people carry out, consciously or unconsciously, in order to produce the adaptations to novel situations which are typical of any complex skill. The ability to use one's car-driving rules to develop a new combination of feet and hand movements when faced with a strange car is comparable to the use of generative rules to produce novel sentences.

If the foregoing arguments are accepted, it is clear that Chomsky's theory provided a major impetus in getting psycholinguistics off the ground as a new approach to the study of language carrying with it general implications for other types of cognitive functioning. Obviously this assessment of the importance of Chomsky's theory has been made with regard to its impact on psychology rather than its status in linguistics.

Within the discipline of linguistics there are many schools of thought: some fervent supporters of transformational grammar, some propounding other types of generative theory and some opposed to the whole notion of generative rules.

However, in the interests of following up the development of psycholinguistics within psychology, this book will concentrate almost entirely on Chomsky's theory. In order to bring out the direct connections between linguistic theory and psychological experiment, the first part of the book contains an account of Chomsky's generative theory. The second part is concerned with the use and misuse that psychologists have made of his ideas; sometimes, it must be admitted, with the active encouragement of transformational linguists themselves.

Part One
Generative Theory

1 Chomsky's Theory: Basic Assumptions

Introduction

Before launching into details of Chomsky's theory one or two points need to be clarified. The first is that, although by definition the interest of Chomsky's theory for psycholinguists lies in its psychological implications, to gain any insight into what the theory is all about, it is essential to keep two aspects entirely distinct. One is the question of why Chomsky's proposals, unlike previous linguistic theories, were taken up by psychologists as having direct relevance to language behaviour. The other is the need to suspend all psychological judgements while attempting to grasp the basic principles of a theory which is a theory of linguistics, not of psychology. Failure to appreciate this has led many a bemused psychologist to feel that the details of Chomsky's system are gratuitously arbitrary. This is not to say that Chomsky himself is not interested in the psychological implications of his theory. Indeed, he has made far-reaching claims about its significance for the study of cognitive processes. However, much of the argument about the validity of these claims rests on the extent to which purely linguistic assumptions hold for models of language behaviour. My aim in the following chapters, therefore, is to present a brief account of Chomsky's theory, concentrating on those aspects that have most interested psychologists, but ignoring for the moment any psychological implications that have been drawn by Chomsky and others. In Part Two full weight will be given to the psychological point of view, necessitating further consideration of some of the problems which have already been touched upon in the introductory chapter.

A second point is that Chomsky's theory is a rapidly developing one. Since the publication of *Syntactic Structures* in 1957, his ideas have undergone many changes, some of them involving apparently radical reformulations. These constant revisions, which have made many people despair of keeping up to date, raise a special problem when it comes to describing the theory. Is it more satisfactory to give the theory in its most recent form or should account be taken of its development? I have adopted the second 'historical' approach for two reasons: one is that by progressing from the simpler, earlier, versions the theory will, it is hoped, become easier to understand and the motivation for subsequent changes more obvious. Secondly, the reactions of psychologists to the various stages can be usefully distinguished. Indeed, it would often be impossible to understand the hypotheses drawn from the theory unless one knew which version was current at the time.

It should be noted, however, that many of the apparent revisions are really clarifications of points which, for one reason or another, had been misunderstood by Chomsky's readers. This is particularly true of Chomsky's discussion of the aims of linguistic theories. In his later books he restated the ideas put forward in *Syntactic Structures*, sometimes using different terms in the attempt to achieve clarity. Nevertheless, the theoretical basis for his linguistic theory has remained constant. Indeed, one of Chomsky's contributions has been to bring into the open the dependence of ostensibly technical procedures such as writing grammars on prior theoretical assumptions. For this reason it is essential to grasp Chomsky's views about the aims of linguistic theories if one is to understand his own grammatical theory.

Aims of linguistic theories

At the practical level of 'what do linguists do?' one answer would be that they produce grammars of natural human languages. But in order to do this they have to subscribe to some general theory of what constitutes a grammar. In 1957 Chomsky proposed that the grammar of a language is like a scientific theory. It is based on a finite number of observations, in this case the corpus of utterances by native speakers recorded by the linguist. However, like any other scientific hypothesis, its aim is to discover generalizations which will also predict all other utterances that could be produced by a speaker of the language.

Such a formulation presupposes that there is some method of distinguishing between utterances that are part of a language and those that are not. When a grammatical rule predicts that a certain sequence of words is a valid utterance in a language there must be some way of verifying whether this is so or not. The whole question of what counts as a 'correct' utterance is by no means as easy as it might appear; it is a problem we shall come back to more than once. However, for the purposes of this theoretical discussion, the assumption is that utterances can be divided into two mutually exclusive classes: sentences (i.e. 'correct' grammatical utterances) and non-sentences (i.e. ungrammatical utterances). A language will be defined as the set of all possible sentences; and the grammar of a language as the rules which distinguish between sentences and non-sentences.

This is simply making explicit an assumption that underlies even the most old-fashioned 'prescriptive' grammar. Prescriptive grammars are those which attempt to lay down some standard of correct usage, such as the 'Queen's English', as opposed to modern descriptive grammars which are concerned with language as it is actually spoken. However, in both cases anyone who follows the rules of a grammar will produce sentences that are considered correct by the grammar and will avoid incorrect utterances not allowed by the grammar.

In *Syntactic Structures* Chomsky drew attention to another quality of the set of possible sentences that constitute a language. This is that the number of such sentences is infinite. There is no way of setting a limit, except in some arbitrary way, to the number of possible sentences. To take a simple example, if one attempted to list all English sentences, it would always be possible to produce new sentences by joining any two sentences using a conjunction such as '*and*' or '*but*'. Similarly, in English the rules for embedding dependent clauses set no theoretical limit on the number of times such embeddings may be carried out; as in the following examples: *The rat ran, The rat the cat chased ran, The rat the cat the dog teased chased ran,*

The rat the cat the dog the man kicked teased chased ran, and so on. This may be a good point at which to remind you that the discussion in this part of the book takes no account of psychological plausibility. The fact that a sentence with, say, ten dependent clauses is unlikely to be spoken and would be impossible to understand at first hearing does not detract from Chomsky's argument that a recursive (i.e. infinitely repeatable) rule of embedding must, in principle, be allowed for in English grammar. Clearly, it would be arbitrary to say that embeddings can only be carried out three times or that sentences can only be of a certain length.

If it were not for this infinite characteristic of language, a grammar could consist merely of a list of the finite number of grammatical sentences. Obviously, such a grammar would be trivially uninformative about the structure of the language concerned. Chomsky's point is that it would not in any case be a viable grammar because it would necessarily leave out an infinite number of possible sentences. It would not, therefore, fulfil the aim of distinguishing between sentences and non-sentences. Taking this into account, a language can be re-defined as the infinite set of grammatical sentences in that language.

From this it follows that a grammar must be projective. This means that it must contain rules that will generate all the infinite number of possible grammatical sentences and no ungrammatical utterances. As we shall see in Part Two, Chomsky's use of the term 'generate' has led to considerable confusion, particularly in connection with attempts to derive behavioural models from the theory. The sense in which he uses it is equivalent to the way a mathematician talks about a formula generating a series of numbers. Similarly, grammatical rules are capable of generating sequences of words or sounds that are consequently defined as correct sentences by the grammar. In principle, this has nothing to do with the way a particular person might produce a particular sentence.

In spite of the fact that Chomsky's theory is often labelled generative grammar, the basic assumption is one that under-lies all grammars. Even the more traditional grammars do not attempt to list all possible sentences. Instead they specify rules or paradigms that indicate the 'correct' forms for sentences. From these, other sentences can be produced. The difference in Chomsky's case is that, because he explicitly emphasized the generative feature of grammars, he was led to formulate his own grammatical rules in a radically novel way.

Evaluation of grammars

One of Chomsky's purposes in discussing the aims of linguistic theories is to establish criteria by which grammars can be evaluated. Chomsky proposes that there are several levels of adequacy to which a grammar can attain, depending on the aims it sets out to fulfil. A linguistic theory will be judged according to the adequacy of the grammars it provides for natural languages.

The first, and weakest, requirement of a grammar follows naturally from the discussion in the previous section: it must be able to distinguish between grammatical and ungrammatical utterances. Furthermore, for the reasons given in the previous section, this cannot be limited to a particular sample of utterances. It must provide rules which will predict which of all possible as yet unheard utterances are grammatical and which not. Chomsky emphasizes that this is an empirical matter, equivalent to scientific predictions about observable facts. The question then arises: what are the empirical data in the case of language? The obvious answer is utterances produced by native speakers. However, it is a well-known fact that people often talk ungrammatically, leaving their sentences half finished, changing their minds in the middle, and so on. What linguists are really after is the set of utterances that an 'idealized' native speaker would accept as being grammatical.

Obviously, operational techniques for collecting such data are of crucial importance to linguists faced with the problem of recording the possible utterances of native speakers of some obscure tribal language. For an understanding of Chomsky's theory it is, perhaps fortunately, unnecessary to go further into this question. The data Chomsky uses for testing his own theories is primarily English – of the East Coast of the United

States variety. What he relies on is his intuitive knowledge about his native language. The assumption is that he and his readers will be in agreement about the distinction between grammatical and ungrammatical English.

This reliance on intuition may sound unscientific, but I think it can be fairly claimed that this way of collecting observations is not subject to the criticisms that are normally levelled against data based on introspection. It does not rely on one man's interpretation but on a general agreement about what constitutes grammatical English. While there may well be arguments about this (for instance, about dialects and stylistic variations), the data cannot be manipulated to fit in with any particular grammatical theory. In this sense the evidence used to evaluate grammars is objective.

Assuming, therefore, that the distinction between grammatical and ungrammatical utterances can be objectively determined the first requirement of a grammar is that its rules should be capable of generating all and only grammatical sentences. Chomsky calls this *weak generative capacity*, and the level of adequacy attained by the grammar *observational adequacy*.

There are two ways in which a grammar could fail even this weakest requirement. The first is that the grammar is not stated in sufficiently explicit terms for it to be put to empirical test. Chomsky would argue that traditional grammars merely specify general paradigms for typical sentences, leaving it to the speaker to use his own intuition about how the rules should be applied to produce other sentences. Since this process itself relies on the speaker's intuitive knowledge of the language, the results will obviously turn out to be intuitively correct sentences. The only real test, therefore, of a grammar is to devise a set of formal rules which, if fed to a computer operating with no prior knowledge of the language, would still be capable of generating only correct grammatical sentences.

Having met this first condition of explicit formalization, the second way in which a grammar could fail the test of observational adequacy would be if it then failed to generate all possible correct sentences and/or generated some ungrammatical utterances. One example of such a grammar would be an attempt to list all possible sentences. Since the set of possible sentences is infinite (as pointed out earlier), such a grammar would automatically fail to meet the criterion of observational adequacy. Chomsky argues also that various probability models of grammar are incapable of generating all possible grammatical sentences in natural languages (for mathematical proofs see Miller and Chomsky, 1963). They are not, therefore, adequate even at the level of observational adequacy.

Chomsky's view is that it is only at the next level of adequacy, which he calls *descriptive adequacy*, that a grammatical theory can begin to be taken seriously. The point Chomsky emphasizes is that there may be several sets of grammatical rules that would succeed in generating all the correct sentences of a language and no non-sentences. All these grammars would have the necessary weak generative capacity. Chomsky introduces the concept of *strong generative capacity* to distinguish grammars that are not only capable of generating all possible sentences, but can also assign correct structural descriptions to the sentences they generate. By structural descriptions Chomsky means that the grammar must assign to each sentence an indication of the structure of the sentence. This involves showing how sentences can be divided into units and sub-units (e.g. subject and predicate and verbs and nouns) and how these units are related to each other. The existence of such structuring makes it possible to indicate the linguistic rationale for the distinction between sentences and non-sentences. It also allows for generalizations which specify how sentences are related to each other.

The correctness of the structural descriptions assigned by a grammar can be judged by whether they accord with a native speaker's intuition as earlier defined. For example, an English speaker knows that the rules for expressing the tense of a verb are related in the sense that one chooses from a set of possible auxiliaries and/or inflections. A grammar which gave separate *ad hoc* rules for Present, Past, Future, etc. without any indication that they were a mutually exclusive set of related possibilities would run counter to any intuitive knowledge of the language. In later chapters arguments of this kind will be cited in support of transformational grammar, based on its superiority in providing structural descriptions which reveal underlying relationships that accord with linguistic intuition.

One might have thought that the requirements of weak and strong generative capacity were sufficiently stringent for the evaluation of grammars. Chomsky goes on to consider a third and higher level of adequacy, that of *explanatory adequacy*. He argues that it is theoretically possible for there to be a variety of descriptively adequate grammars all of which, although based on different principles, have the strong generative capacity of producing correct structural descriptions for the sentences of a language. The concept underlying explanatory adequacy is that there is in fact one best type of grammar which can be selected out of all possible descriptively adequate grammars. The way in which Chomsky defines this 'best' grammar strikes an odd note in the context of the discussion up to this point, since he relates it to the child's acquisition of language. He points out that the child is faced with the same sort of task as the linguist. He hears certain utterances, which Chomsky calls primary linguistic data. From this he has to devise a set of rules which will not only account for the sample of speech to which he is exposed but will also be capable of generating new sentences. This is the same as saying that the child has to develop a theory about the grammar of the language he is learning. Chomsky claims that, out of all the many possible grammars which are compatible with the incoming data, all children choose one particular type of grammar. From this he deduces that children must have some sort of innate linguistic ability which enables them to choose the one type of grammar which is most appropriate for analysing language in general; the actual content of the grammar will naturally vary according to the particular language to which the child is exposed.

The extent to which this is a plausible account of how a child actually learns his mother tongue is a question for empirical study. The point Chomsky is making here is that, if there is one appropriate type of grammatical analysis which all children are programmed to develop, then it must be universal to all languages. This universal grammatical theory would give an account of the grammatical forms and relations that are common to all languages, which Chomsky calls *linguistic universals*. Grammars of individual languages would need to include only the specific rules and content of a language which differentiate it from other languages.

Chomsky is saying that, if a linguistic theory is content with achieving descriptive adequacy, it will be able to produce descriptively adequate grammars for particular natural languages. Alternatively, a theory can aim at explanatory adequacy. This would mean that it attempts to provide a systematic account of language in general which would allow it, like the child, to pick out the one best type of descriptively adequate grammar for any language on the basis of universal features of language.

One final question remains. What are the objective criteria for deciding whether a grammar is of the type that a child is innately predisposed to look for? Unlike the cases of observational and descriptive adequacy, which are judged against the intuitive knowledge of the adult native speaker, one can hardly ask a child what sort of grammatical theory he is geared to produce. Chomsky's formulation of explanatory adequacy in these terms has led many psychologists to concentrate on studying the grammatical systems developed by children as they start learning to speak. An alternative strategy which has interested linguists is to study languages in all parts of the world with a view to discovering linguistic universals common to them all which can plausibly be considered to be part of every child's linguistic equipment.

Chomsky's own analysis of language has relied mainly on the concept of what he calls significant generalizations. The idea is that the rules of a grammar must be formulated in a way that results in the largest number of features of the language being accounted for by the fewest number of generalizations. The more apparent irregularities in a language explainable by rules which show systematic underlying regularities (thus reducing the need for a proliferation of *ad hoc* exceptions), the more adequate the grammar. This criterion is similar to the one used by scientists to distinguish between two theories both of which account for the observed facts. An example is the Ptolemaic and Copernician theories about the movement of the heavenly bodies. Copernicus' theory has triumphed because it was able to give an explanation of the apparent irregularities of their orbits using more powerful generalizations that required less *ad hoc* assumptions.

The idea behind Chomsky's use of this principle is presumably that the one type of grammar all children develop on the basis of primary linguistic data will be the one that provides the most economical grammatical analysis of their language. Moreover, because of the postulated universality of the child's innate linguistic equipment, grammars should be judged not just by the economy with which they express the rules of a particular language. Further savings can be made by discovering generalizations that account for features universal to all languages, since these do not have to be restated in the grammars of individual languages.

However, since we are still a long way off from having a universal theory of language, it is by no means easy in practice to judge which selection of rules will result in the most economical statement of grammatical relations. Length of grammar has been suggested as a criterion but there are many difficulties about this depending on the notation used. For instance, is a grammar with a small number of long rules more economical than one with a large number of short rules?

In fact, when Chomsky is arguing the merits of rival grammatical formulations he appeals once again to a shared intuitive knowledge about which rules account for more underlying regularities of language. His method is to show by examples how a single general rule can relate a set of apparently unconnected grammatical constructions which would previously have required several separate rules. It is undeniable that this method of exposition sometimes induces in the reader a faintly dissatisfied feeling that one might be able to think of counterexamples which would highlight other relationships and necessitate either different or more complicated rules. Indeed, Chomsky's own habit of discovering new examples of obscure

grammatical connections is one of the factors that has contri-
buted to the constant refinements of his basic theory. It must
be remembered, however, that the final aim is to produce
a grammar that will account for all possible examples and
counter-examples of utterances. Also, despite all appearances
to the contrary, the purpose of these theoretical revisions is to
make grammars simpler, by using the fewest possible rules to
express the full complexity of grammatical relations.

Summary

A *language* is defined as the infinite set of grammatical sentences in a language.

A *grammar* is a finite set of rules that will generate this infinite set of grammatical sentences and no non-sentences.

Levels of adequacy

Chomsky's theory proposes that grammars can be judged against three levels of adequacy. Each level presupposes the previous ones. As the requirements get more stringent more possible grammars are eliminated until at the third and final level only one type of grammar fulfills all the criteria.

1. *Observational adequacy.* A grammar must have *weak generative capacity*, i.e. it must provide precisely formulated rules that will generate the infinite set of possible sentences in a language and no non-sentences.

Empirical data: idealized native speakers' intuitions about what constitutes a correct grammatical sentence.

2. *Descriptive adequacy.* A grammar must also have *strong generative capacity*, i.e. it must provide rules that assign correct structural descriptions to the sentences it generates.

Empirical data: idealized native speakers' intuitions about structural relations between sentences.

3. *Explanatory adequacy.* A grammar must assign structural descriptions that are in accordance with a theory of *linguistic universals*. The assumption is that all children have an innate predisposition to develop this one universal type of grammar for their native language.

Empirical data: idealized native speakers' intuitions about which grammatical rules allow the most features of all languages to be accounted for by the fewest number of underlying generalizations.

2 Chomsky's Theory: 1957 Version

Introduction

This chapter will describe the version of Chomsky's theory that appeared in his first book, *Syntactic Structures*. The book covers a wide diversity of topics including the goals of linguistic theories and criteria for evaluating grammars. Here, we are concerned with the actual system of grammatical rules proposed by Chomsky. However, the aims of the grammar and the supporting evidence are based on the theoretical assumptions discussed in the previous chapter.

The basic proposal in *Syntactic Structures* is that the system of grammatical rules for generating sentences and assigning structural descriptions should consist of three parts: phrase structure rules, transformational rules and morphophonemic rules. These will be described in the next three sections, followed by a final section evaluating the system in relation to the criteria of adequacy set out in the last chapter.

Phrase structure rules

This part of the grammar consists of a set of rewriting rules. The easiest way to make this notion clear is to give an example of how a small section of the grammar might be formulated.

1.	S (Sentence)	→ NP (noun phrase) + VP (verb phrase)
2.	NP	→ art (article) + N (noun)
3.	NP	→ N
4.	VP	→ V (verb) + NP
5.	VP	→ V
6.	VP	→ V + adj (adjective)
7.	N	→ *Jane, boy, dog, dogs*, etc.
8.	V	→ *likes, hits, hit, came, was*, etc.
9.	adj	→ *good, unfortunate*, etc.
10.	art	→ *a, the*

These rules indicate that each symbol on the left hand of an arrow can be replaced, or rewritten, by the symbol or symbols on the right hand side. Starting with the original axiom (S for sentence), and continuing to rewrite until you end up with terminal symbols which cannot be rewritten (in this case, words), several grammatical sentences can be generated even by this tiny fragment of grammar. The way in which these rules operate can be demonstrated most clearly by a tree diagram such as that shown in Figure 1. At each level the symbols at the previous level are rewritten according to the rules. Thus, the sentence *Jane likes the dog* is generated by applying the following rules:

1. S   → NP + VP
3. NP   → N
4. VP   → V + NP
2. NP   → art + N
7. N   → *Jane*
8. V   → *likes*
10. art   → *the*
7. N   → *dog*

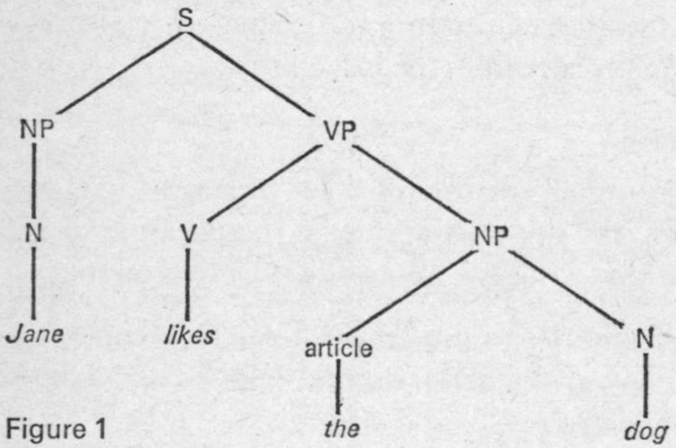

Figure 1

Other sentences that could be generated by the same grammar are:

Jane hits the boy
The dog likes the boy
A boy likes Jane
Jane was unfortunate

You may be interested to work out the appropriate tree diagrams for these sentences.

Tree diagrams of this kind are not merely a handy way of demonstrating the operation of the rules. More importantly, they represent structural descriptions of the sentences generated by the grammar. These structural descriptions (or phrase markers as they are called in Chomsky's theory) specify the structure of the sentence in terms of its generative history. In other words, they show how the sentence has been derived by following the rules of the grammar. Note, however, that, apart from the condition that for any one branch of the tree, symbols at higher levels must be rewritten first, the tree diagram phrase marker does not indicate the order in which the rules have been applied. In the example given above, Rule 1 has to be applied first and, for instance, Rule 4 has to be applied before Rule 8. On the other hand, it is immaterial whether Rule 7 is applied before or after Rule 4. The correct ordering of rules is one of the most difficult problems when it comes to writing complex grammars which can generate a wider range of sentences.

Another complication is the question of whether the re-writing rules should be context-free or context-sensitive. In the former case the rules indicate that the left hand symbol can always be replaced by the right hand symbols regardless of the context. But there are many aspects of even such simple sentences as we are discussing that could be more conveniently specified if the rules were restricted to certain contexts. An example would be the need to indicate whether a verb should be rewritten in the singular or plural form, as in *Jane runs* or *The boys run*. One way of dealing with this would be to include in the grammar context-sensitive rules such as:

$$NP \rightarrow \begin{cases} NP \text{ sing} \\ \text{or} \\ NP \text{ plural} \end{cases}$$

Verb → *runs*/in the context: NP sing + ——
Verb → *run*/in the context: NP plural + ——

In effect this is saying that the symbol for Verb should be re-written as *runs* in the context of a singular noun phrase (e.g., *Jane*) and by *run* in the context of a plural noun phrase (e.g. *The boys*), although the actual rules for achieving this are, of course, much more general and complex.

Perhaps the most important aspect of the rewriting rules is that they are purely formal. They do not in any way rely on an intuitive sense of what a sentence is. The idea is that, if a machine started with S and continued picking at random from among the various alternative ways of rewriting each symbol, all the resulting strings of words would be grammatical English sentences. The aim of a full grammar would be to make it possible to generate all possible English sentences and avoid generating any impermissible strings of words. At the same time, the grammar would automatically generate structural descriptions in the form of tree diagram phrase markers for each sentence.

It may have struck the reader that these tree diagrams look very like the parsing of sentences traditionally carried out by grammarians. In both cases the sentence is divided into a hier-archy of units and sub-units. Much of the work of modern linguistics has been concerned with devising formal procedures for carrying out this type of analysis known as *immediate constituent analysis*. At each level units are classified as the immediate constituents of the units at the next level. Thus in Figure 1 the units art and N are immediate constituents of the unit NP, V and NP are in turn immediate constituents of VP, and VP and the left hand NP are immediate constituents of the sentence itself. Clearly, this is closely parallel to parsing a sentence into subject (NP) and predicate (VP), and then going on to subdivide the predicate into verb and noun phrase, and so on.

The novelty of Chomsky's approach lies in the form of rules he uses to express this information. By aiming to provide a set of rewriting rules that will generate an infinite number of sen-tence phrase markers, he emphasises that it is not sufficient for linguists to be able to analyse the constituents of a limited sample of sentences. The role of a grammar is to generate structural descriptions for all possible sentences that could be produced by a speaker of the language. As will be seen in Part Two, this implied contrast between Chomsky's dynamic generative rules and the static nature of constituent analysis played a major part in awakening psychologists' interest in Chomsky's theory. But from a purely linguistic point of view, the important thing is that the same information about the heirarchical structure of sentences is conveyed by constituent analysis as by phrase structure rules. It is not until one moves on to transformational rules that a radically different kind of linguistic analysis emerges.

Transformational rules

The assumption behind immediate constituent analysis is that all sentences can be directly analysed into a hierarchy of constituent units. In the course of his attempt to produce a set of formal rewriting rules which would generate all possible phrase structure hierarchies, Chomsky came to the conclusion that the rule system could be radically simplified if another kind of rule were allowed. The introduction of transformational rules is central to Chomsky's theory; so much so that grammars of this type are known as transformational grammars.

The first essential is to grasp the exact difference between phrase structure and transformational rules. The basic feature of transformational rules is that they operate not on single symbols but on *strings* of symbols. Phrase structure rules of the kind given in the previous section provide for the rewriting of individual symbols, each operation being applied in isolation. Thus by Rule 4 on page 35, whenever the symbol VP appears it can be rewritten as V + NP regardless of the rewriting of any other symbols. Transformational rules, on the other hand, take into account the way in which the other symbols in a string have been rewritten.

In *Syntactic Structures* this is achieved by making transformational rules apply to the terminal strings output by the phrase structure rules. This means that transformational rules can be formulated so that they apply only to certain strings of symbols, as indicated by the phrase structure tree diagram showing how symbols have been rewritten. A grossly over-simplified example would be a transformational rule which performs a reordering operation on any string with the structure NP + *was* + adj, transforming it into adj + *was* + NP (for symbols and abbreviations see page 35). This would mean that the string of symbols underlying the sentence *Jane was unfortunate* would be reordered into the string underlying *Unfortunate was Jane*. But even such a simple reversal rule could not be applied to *any* string of three symbols. If it were, the string art + N + VP could be reordered as VP + N + art, allowing a string such as *The cat runs* to be turned into *Runs cat the*. By specifying the structural description of the strings to which transformational rules can apply, their operation is limited to strings which have the appropriate generative 'history' as embodied in their phrase markers.

The next question to consider is why a grammar that includes transformational rules should be simpler than one in which all sentences are directly generated by phrase structure rewriting rules. The basic reason is that any serious attempt to generate all but the most simple of sentences immediately comes up against the problem that the selection of individual words in a sentence depends on what other words have already been selected. Among numerous examples are the matching of nouns and verbs for number and gender, selection of appropriate pronouns to stand in for nouns, choosing a direct object when the verb is transitive, preventing choice of an inanimate subject such as *sincerity* with a 'human' verb such as *admired*, and so on. To ignore these interdependencies between words would lead to the generation of many incorrect sentences. While it is possible to deal with some of them by context-sensitive rewriting rules of the kind described on page 37, it is clear that a type of rule which makes the final form of a sentence dependent on its overall phrase structure makes possible a more economical statement of such interdependencies.

A pertinent illustration is afforded by Chomsky's discussion of the passive construction in *Syntactic Structures*. Suppose one tried to generate passive sentences using rewriting rules that apply to only one symbol at a time. To start off with, one must add the auxiliary verb *to be* and appropriately inflect the main verb, as in *The boy is being bitten by the dog*. Chomsky formulates this rule as one way of rewriting the auxiliary:

aux $\rightarrow be + en$

The next step would be to insert *by* before the second NP, possibly by a rewriting rule:

NP $\rightarrow by + $ NP

The difficulty is that NP can only be rewritten as $by + $ NP in the context of aux already having been rewritten in the passive form; it is not possible to have *by* without the passive form of the verb, in other words, *The boy bites by the dog* is not permissible. But, equally, the rule for rewriting aux. in the passive cannot apply except in the case when $by + $ NP is also selected, because *The boy is being bitten the dog* is also wrong. This sort of interlocking of contexts is very difficult to handle within a system in which individual symbols are rewritten independently of how other rewriting rules have been applied. Specification of context sensitive restrictions would be cumbersome to say the least.

Chomsky argues that the simplest way to deal with these problems is to specify the structure of strings underlying active sentences which can be turned into the passive, and then apply the transformational rule:

$NP_1 + $ aux. $ + V + NP_2 \Rightarrow NP_2 + be + en + V + by + NP_1$

This provides for the simultaneous introduction of $be + en$ and $by + $ NP (and, at the same time, achieves a reduction in the phrase structure section of the grammar which no longer has to include rules for rewriting aux as $be + en$ and NP as $by + $ NP). The form of the transformational rule means that any string with the structure on the left hand side can be turned into an equivalent passive version. For example, *The dog chases the cat* becomes *The cat is being chased by the dog* and *The boy bites Jane* becomes *Jane is being bitten by the boy*.

An important point is that the structural description of the string to be transformed can be expressed in terms of symbols occurring at any level of the hierarchy, as long as these symbols add up to a complete analysis of the string at some level. For example: in the case of the passive transformation, it is obviously economical to work at the level of NP units, rather than having to take into account all the possible combinations of symbols into which NP might be divided. In its present form the transformation applies equally to *Jane likes Bill* and *The very small boy was chasing the black cat*, since it applies to any string which can be analysed as containing units corresponding to NP_1 and NP_2. If this were not the case, separate transformations would have to be formulated for strings of the form: N + aux + V + N, art + N + aux + V + N, art + adj + N + aux + V + art + N, and so on. What is required is a specification of the minimum structure common to all active strings that can be turned into the passive; in this case NP_1 and NP_2 being the right level of analysis. On the other hand, a structural description of the form NP + VP would be too unspecific because the passive transformation can only apply when VP has been rewritten as V + NP_2, indicating that the sentence has a transitive verb and direct object.

Another gain from the above formulation is that any restriction that might apply to the choice of subject (NP_1) and object (NP_2) in the active sentence is automatically reproduced in the passive by switching round NP_1 and NP_2. If the grammar allows the generation of *John admires sincerity* as an acceptable string but not *Sincerity admires John*, then reordering NP_1 and NP_2 would allow the passive *Sincerity is admired by John* but not *John is admired by sincerity*. As Chomsky points out, if one tried to generate passives directly, all such restrictions would have to be restated in the opposite direction for passive sentences, since with any direct rewriting system NP_1 and NP_2 would remain in their original positions, producing *John + be + en + admired + by + sincerity*.

I have gone into the case for the passive transformation in some detail, in spite of the fact that this transformation underwent further revisions in Chomsky's later work. The reason for this is to demonstrate that, despite their apparent complexity, transformations are more powerful than phrase structure rules. By operating on the overall structures of strings, they allow considerable simplification of the rules required to produce the full range of grammatical sentences.

Based on such considerations, Chomsky's conclusion is that the simplest grammar will consist of both phrase structure rules, which directly generate a limited set of underlying strings, and transformational rules, which perform permutation, deletion and addition operations on these strings to produce all the possible sentences in a language. Some of the transformational rules are *optional*, as in the case of the passive transformation discussed above, and a whole range of similar transformations such as negatives and questions. In addition to these, there are also *obligatory* transformations, which arose from Chomsky's demonstration that certain compulsory syntactic features (e.g., agreement between number of subject and verb, introduction of the element *do* into negatives and questions, and insertion of word boundaries) are simpler if treated as transformations taking into account the overall structure of the sentence.

There is a final group of transformations which Chomsky calls *generalized tranformations*. In contrast to the transformations so far described (which are *singulary* in that they apply to a single underlying string), these are used to join strings underlying two or more sentences so as to produce compound and complex sentences. The simplest case is conjunction, when two sentences are joined together by *and* or *but*. However, generalized transformations are required also when one string is embedded into another as a dependent clause. For example, the sentence *The girl who is unloved bit John* or, for that matter, *The unloved girl bit John*, would both result from a combination of two underlying strings *The girl is unloved* and *The girl bit John*. Obviously, all generalized transformations come into the category of optional transformations.

From this distinction between obligatory and optional transformations, Chomsky went on to define a subset of sentences which makes up the kernel of a language. It was the concept of kernel sentences which originally attracted most attention from psychologists. It is important, therefore, to understand just what Chomsky meant by this. In *Syntactic Structures* the kernel of a language is defined as the set of sentences which are produced by applying only obligatory transformations to the strings generated by the phrase structure component of the grammar. In effect these would be simple, active, affirmative, declarative sentences to which only such obligatory transformations as number agreement, correct placement of auxiliaries and so on have to be applied. All other sentences would be the result of applying optional transformations, whether the latter are singularly (such as the passive, negative and interrogative operating on a single string), or generalized (such as the rules for conjoining sentences and embedding dependent clauses). Since further transformations can be carried out on already transformed strings, there is no theoretical limit to the complexity of sentences that can be generated.

A final point is that Chomsky makes it clear that transformations do not apply to kernel sentences as such but to the structure of the strings underlying them as specified by the phrase structure rules. However, as we shall see, it was the vivid terminology of kernel sentences being transformed into complex sentences that was taken up by psychologists. This led to considerable confusion in regard to Chomsky's later formalizations of basically the same principle.

Morphophonemic rules

This section of the grammar is treated very briefly in *Syntactic Structures*. The reason for its existence is to provide a set of rules for turning the symbols in terminal strings into a representation of their actual spoken form. For convenience of exposition the terminal strings of both phrase structure and transformational rules have been treated as if they consisted of actual words; this is generally true of the examples given in *Syntactic Structures*.

Strictly, however, the units in terminal strings are what linguists call *morphemes*. These are defined as the minimal units of grammatical analysis. They need not necessarily be complete words since some words are made up of two or more morphemes. *Singer* can be analysed as containing two morphemes *sing* and *er*, the *er* being the same as the morpheme that occurs in *dancer*, *baker*, and *writer* but different from the *er* in *bigger* and *smaller*. Similarly, in *runs* the *s* can be thought of as a '3rd person singular present' morpheme, or if the word is taken as a noun a 'plural' morpheme. Naturally, there are many difficulties linguists have to deal with such as irregular plurals like *men* or *sheep* in which the plural morpheme cannot be isolated as such.

At the level of grammatical analysis it is more convenient to work with grammatical morphemes such as 'past' and 'present', 'singular' and 'plural', independently of the actual form they would take when applied to different words. At this level it is only their grammatical implications that are important. In order to formulate a number agreement rule, it is necessary only to indicate whether the subject and verb should both be singular or plural, the question of whether the final word will follow regular rules, such as adding *s* for the plural, or will be irregular, such as *men*, being irrelevant.

Chomsky's proposed morphophonemic rules are designed to convert these abstract morphemes into the actual phonetic sounds contained in the spoken sentence. At the time of *Syntactic Structures* he followed the established practice of expressing this phonetic level in terms of *phonemes*. The usual definition is that phonemes are the phonetic sounds needed to make distinctions between words (or more strictly between morphemes) in a particular language. Thus, in English the sounds *b* and *v* are different phonemes, because they distinguish *ban* from *van* and other similar pairs. However, the *k* sounds in *cat* and *cool*, though different sounds phonetically, are regarded as the same phoneme in English because there is no case of two words which are distinguished solely by this contrast. The interesting thing is that to non-linguistically trained English speakers these two *k*s psychologically sound identical despite their articulatory and acoustic differences. In other languages the *b* and *v* contrast performs no distinguishing function and, as a result, is not normally differentiated by native speakers. And there are languages that use tone as a functional phonetic feature, a whole dimension that is irrelevant and so 'unheard' in English.

The very few morphophonemic rules given in *Syntactic Structures* involve the rewriting of lexical and grammatical morphemes to give a phonemic description of the sounds involved:

take + past → /tuk/
hit + past → /hit/
past → /d/
take → /teyk/

Chomsky noted that, in spite of being in the form of rewriting rules, these rules differ from phrase structure rules in allowing more than one symbol to be rewritten at a time. Similar morphographemic rules would be necessary to convert terminal strings into their correctly spelt written form.

The sketchiness of the morphophonemic rules reflects the fact that at this stage Chomsky appears to have added them only for the sake of completeness. In the course of developing the phonological component of the later version of his theory he came to radically different conclusions about the validity of the traditional categories of morphemes and phonemes.

Evaluation

The aim of this section is to consider how the 1957 version of transformational grammar meets the criteria of adequacy outlined on page 34. First, to summarize the system: the transformational grammar proposed in *Syntactic Structures* accounts for the generation of sentences in several stages. To begin with, the phrase structure rewriting rules generate a set of terminal strings, the structural descriptions of which can be expressed as hierarchical tree diagrams of the kind shown in Figure 1. The output of the phrase structure rules is limited to strings which directly underly kernel sentences, i.e. those simple sentences which require only obligatory transformations, and, of course, appropriate morphophonemical rules, to arrive at their final phonetic representation. All other more complex sentences are the result of a series of optional transformations being applied to phrase structure terminal strings, which in turn may bring into force further obligatory transformations. Finally, these strings produced by optional transformations, including generalized transformations for combining strings, are processed by the morphophonemic rules. Chomsky points out that, once such a division of rules has been accepted, the linguist is able to make choices about a set of phrase structure rules which will allow the simplest direct generation of kernel sentences; and, at the same time, enable transformations to operate with the greatest amount of generality (as, for example, by using the same rules to introduce auxiliaries like *do* into both negatives and questions).

To consider first the lowest level of weak generative capacity, how does transformational grammar measure up to the requirement of being able to generate all the sentences in a language and no non-sentences? Since transformational rules are more powerful than previous proposals the question takes the form of whether a weaker grammar, such as a context-free phrase structure grammar, could in fact achieve equal weak generative power. One of Chomsky's co-workers Paul Postal (1964) has demonstrated that certain grammatical constructions in Mohawk cannot be handled by a context-free phrase structure system. Whether such sentences could be generated by phrase structure rules which do specify context restrictions is an arguable point, but in the case of Mohawk, Postal calculates that several millions of context-sensitive rules would be necessary to generate certain constructions. The example of the passive construction given earlier highlights the difficulty of expressing contextual interdependencies within a framework of phrase structure rules for rewriting individual symbols.

Further, Chomsky argues, even if equivalent weak capacity to generate sentences were granted, there are still many important facts about language that cannot be explained in purely phrase structure terms. One example of this is the ambiguity to a speaker of English of a sentence like *The shooting of the hunters was awful*. This would be given the same phrase structure analysis into immediate constituents, regardless of whether the hunters were taken as the subject or object of the verb *shoot*. Transformationally, however, the difference between the two possible interpretations could be expressed by deriving the first noun phrase from different underlying kernel strings: *The hunters shoot* or *Someone shoots the hunters*. This type of argument is the forerunner of Chomsky's later definition of descriptive adequacy as the requirement that a grammar should have the strong generative capacity of being able to generate structural descriptions that are in accordance with native speakers' intuitions. Another case would be the linking of a simple kernel sentence with related sentences by transformations such as the passive, negative and interrogative. This squares with the intuitive feeling that the sentences *Mary is hitting John, John is being hit by Mary, Mary is not hitting John* and *Is Mary hitting John?* are in some way related. On these grounds, transformational rules would be more highly valued than the many independent and *ad hoc* rules that would be needed to generate these sentences in a phrase structure grammar.

In *Syntactic Structures* Chomsky discusses the possibility that reliance on native speakers' understanding of ambiguous meanings might be taken as indicating that grammars should be based on semantic considerations. He argues strongly against this on the grounds that there is no one-to-one relationship between grammatical rules and semantic concepts. For instance, the grammatical subject does not always refer to an agent, as in *John received a blow on the head*. Again, although it happens that actives and passives generally have the same meaning, any attempt to specify transformations in terms of synonymity would have prevented insights into the structural relations between affirmatives and negatives.

The requirement that structural descriptions produced by the grammar must match the native speaker's intutions about meaning relationships does not mean that such intuitions can be used as a substitute for formal generative rules. It is rather that the rules must be able to provide a formal basis for explaining the way in which people intuitively understand sentences. Indeed, it can be argued that Chomsky's theoretical position is the reverse of basing grammar on meaning. On the contrary, the implication is that prior grammatical analysis is a necessary condition for explaining meaning relationships, a notion that is at the core of Chomsky's treatment of syntax and semantics in the 1965 version of his theory.

Finally, there is the third level of explanatory adequacy; this being the requirement that grammatical rules should be in accordance with a universal theory of language in order to account for how children develop adequate grammars for their various native languages. As indicated earlier, the criterion for judging explanatory adequacy is that a grammatical theory should account for the greatest number of features of natural languages by the fewest underlying generalizations. Particularly favoured are those that simplify grammars of individual languages by specifying rules that are universal to all languages. In *Syntactic Structures* this criterion is reflected in Chomsky's concern to show that the introduction of transformational rules results in a much simpler grammar by providing general rules that cover more types of sentences. Although he admits that the notion of 'simplicity' is vague, in his later work he makes the point that choice of a simplicity measure is itself a hypothesis about the nature of human language. A theory of universal grammar provides the linguist, and the child learner, with 'simplicity' evaluation measures for choosing the most economical system of rules to account for linguistic data. Chomsky's claim is that the division of grammar into phrase structure and transformational rules is a universal feature of language which allows for the development of the greatest number of significant generalizations. But the theory is empirical in the sense that it could be falsified if languages were found for which a transformational analysis did not reveal the underlying generalizations that are necessary for children to master a language system.

Summary

A grammar consists of three types of rules:

1. *Phrase structure rules*, which rewrite individual symbols so as to produce strings represented by hierarchical tree diagrams.

2. *Transformational rules*, which operate on the overall structures of phrase structure strings so as to produce the strings underlying sentences in their final form.

3. *Morphophonemical rules*, which convert the strings produced by transformational rules into the actual sounds of a sentence.

Definition of 'kernel' sentences

Transformational rules can be either *obligatory* or *optional*. If only obligatory transformations are applied, the resulting string will underly a 'kernel' sentence. If both obligatory and optional transformations are applied, strings underlying more complex sentences can be generated. Optional transformations can be either *singular* or *generalized*, i.e. either operate on one 'kernel' string or combine two or more strings.

Levels of adequacy

Compared with a purely phrase structure grammar, transformational grammar meets the three levels of adequacy (see p. 34).

1. It has the *weak generative capacity* of generating an infinite number of sentences.

2. It has the *strong generative capacity* of generating structural descriptions of sentences which match a native speaker's intuitions about relations between sentences.

3. The claim is that transformational grammar achieves *explanatory adequacy* by providing the most economical set of rules for generating natural languages, the form of the rules being universal to all languages.

3 Chomsky's Theory: 1965 Version

Introduction

There has been a tendency among psychologists to treat the later versions of Chomsky's theory as if they represented a radical break with the proposals put forward in *Syntactic Structures*. This is partly because, in an attempt to clear up misunderstandings, Chomsky restated some of the basic notions of the 1957 theory, often using different terminology to express essentially the same idea. Also, whereas his earlier work was more closely confined to linguistic implications, in his later writings Chomsky draws philosophical and psychological conclusions from his theory.

The formulation of the theory discussed in this chapter is that presented in *Aspects of the Theory of Syntax* (1965) and *Topics in the Theory of Generative Grammar* (1966a). One possible source of confusion is that, like the earlier 1957 theory, the 1965 version postulates a three component grammar; but the three components are not identical to those of 1957. In 1965 the division is into a syntactic component, a phonological component and a semantic component. Compared with the earlier version, the phonological component can be thought of as being equivalent to the morphophonemical rules, although the actual form of the rules differ in the two systems. The important point to grasp is that the syntactic component in the 1965 version includes both a set of base rules, roughly equivalent to the 1957 phrase structure rules, and a set of transformational rules. The semantic component is a new addition consisting of rules for semantic interpretation of the meanings of sentences. The following diagram indicates the relation between the two theories.

1957	*1965*
None	Semantic component
Phrase structure rules ⎫	⎧ Base rules
Transformational rules ⎬ Syntactic	⎨ Transformational
⎭ component	⎩ rules
Morphophonemical rules	Phonological component

To add to the difficulties, the base rules of the 1965 syntactic component are further divided into phrase structure rewriting rules and a lexicon. The following sections will describe the general properties of the syntactic component, the lexicon, the semantic component, and the phonological component, ending with a summary and evaluation.

One preliminary point that should be emphasized is the extended definition of what is covered by the term grammar. The 1957 version of transformational grammar was concerned mainly with syntax and, marginally, phonetics. Grammatical rules, therefore, could be taken as virtually synonymous with syntactic rules, thus maintaining the traditional separation of grammar and meaning. However, with the introduction of a semantic component in the 1965 theory, transformational grammar has been extended to include not only syntactic rules for generating the sentences of a language but also semantic rules for assigning meanings to those sentences. In this way transformational grammar sets out to account for the complete linguistic competence of the native speaker, including his ability to produce and understand meaningful sentences.

Syntactic component

The main innovation in the 1965 account of the syntactic component was the introduction of the concepts of deep and surface structure. A similar distinction was already implicit in the 1957 version. There the output of the phrase structure rules consisted of underlying strings which had to be operated on by transformations to produce the final forms of sentences for morphophonemical analysis. In the 1965 theory deep structures are similarly generated by the phrase structure rules included in the base of the syntactic component and are thus equivalent to the underlying strings of the 1957 grammar. As in the earlier version, transformations perform operations on these deep structures in order to map them on to their final form, or surface structure. The major difference is that in the 1957 account a sharp distinction was made between kernel sentences, which require only obligatory transformations, and complex sentences, which are the result of optional transformations. The implication, at least as taken up by psychologists, was that there are two classes of sentences: simple active affirmative declarative kernel sentences directly generated by the phrase structure rules and all other sentences which are produced by transforming and combining kernels.

In the 1965 theory the emphasis is on the fact that every sentence has a deep structure and a surface structure. Moreover, when it comes to the transformations that map deep structures on to surface structures, the distinction between obligatory and optional transformations disappears. The final surface structures of both simple and complex sentences are obligatorily determined by markers in deep structure, which have the function of indicating which transformations are to be put into operation. For example, instead of passives, negatives and questions being the result of optional transformations, their underlying deep structures will contain a passive, negative or question transformation marker.

In the case of generalized transformations for combining strings, the deep structure contains all the underlying strings that will be incorporated into the final sentence. These constituent strings are generated in deep structure by allowing base rules in which the symbol S (for sentence) appears on the right hand side of rewriting rules. Examples would be:

NP → S
NP → that + S

Application of such rules might result in a sentence with the (over-simplified) deep structure shown in Figure 2, termed by Chomsky a generalized phrase marker. Appropriate obligatory transformations would be triggered off according to a specified sequence, starting with the most deeply embedded string and working upwards to produce the final surface structure of the sentence *That the hunters shoot is awful*. This device accounts for the infinite recursiveness of language, since there is no theoretical limit to the number of S strings that can be embedded in a sentence, thus allowing for the generation of an infinite number of sentences.

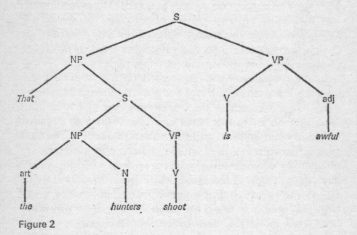

Figure 2

One drawback of abolishing the distinction between obligatory and optional transformations is that the links between kernel and related sentences can no longer be stated in the simple style of the earlier theory. In *Aspects of the Theory of Syntax* Chomsky describes kernel sentences as those which involve 'a minimum of transformational apparatus in their generation', but does not make it clear how this should be defined. All sentences now have deep structures and obligatory transformations which map them on to surface structures; the only way to designate the connection between simple kernel sentences and their related passives, negatives and questions would be by a formula (not yet detailed) specifying the identify of their deep structures apart from the presence or absence of a passive, negative or interrogative marker.

In view of the loss of a clear-cut differentiation between kernel and complex sentences (one of the attractions of Chomsky's 1957 transformational grammar), what are the advantages of the 1965 version? The principal point is that it results in a conceptually simpler organization of the grammar. Paradoxically, the first step in the argument demonstrates the basic similarity between the 1957 and 1965 versions, since the case for deep structures is essentially the same as that for underlying kernel strings. In both cases it is argued that knowledge of the underlying strings that go to make up a sentence is essential for accounting for the native speaker's understanding of similarity and ambiguity relations between sentences. The example of the ambiguous sentence *The shooting of the hunters was awful* discussed on page 47 would still be relevant in terms of the 1965 grammar, since the two interpretations would be represented by different deep structure generalized phrase markers. In one the first noun phrase would be rewritten as *The hunters shoot* and in the other as *Someone shoots the hunters*. The obvious advantage of the 1965 type of generalized phrase marker is that, whereas in the 1957 version such compound sentences had to be produced by rules joining together separate underlying kernel strings, a phrase marker of the type shown in Figure 2 not only includes all the constituent strings but, more importantly, indicates the structural relations that hold between them in the final sentence. In the example given it is clear that the embedded string *The hunters shoot* constitutes part of the subject noun phrase of the complete sentence.

This demonstration of the crucial role of deep structure relations for understanding semantic relation leads to the crucial proposal that deep structures should contain all the information necessary for semantic interpretation of a sentence. This formalizes the requirement that the output of the syntactic component should provide a basis for the native speaker's awareness of semantic relationships. At the same time, the formal separation between syntax and semantics is preserved.

The rules of the syntactic component provide the structural information necessary for semantic interpretation. But it is the rules of the semantic component that carry out a semantic analysis to arrive at the meaning of the sentence.

Exactly matching this concept of deep structure containing all the syntactic information required for semantic interpretation is the equivalent proposal that the surface structure of a sentence contains all the syntactic information necessary for phonological analysis. The complete, and neatly symmetrical, picture is that the syntactic component generates both a deep structure and a surface structure for every sentence. The deep structure is the output of the base rules of the syntactic component and the input to the semantic component; the surface structure is the output of the transformational rules and the input to the phonological component. As shown in Figure 3, analysis by the syntactic component is a prior and necessary precondition for both semantic and phonetic representation. The semantic and phonological components are purely interpretative since they only operate on the output generated by the syntactic component.

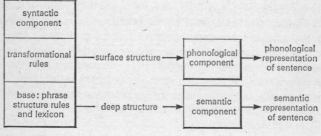

Figure 3

The case for taking deep structures as the basis for semantic interpretation rests on the fact that the phrase structure 'kernel' strings of which they are composed represent the basic grammatical relations that are required to understand the meaning of a sentence. In contrast, these basic subject/object relations are often unclear in surface structure. In the example already mentioned of *The shooting of the hunters was awful* it is only when the surface structure is analysed into two different deep structures that a basis for the ambiguous semantic interpretations is provided. Another example is the often quoted sentences:

John is eager to please
John is easy to please.

These have the same surface structure although in the first John is the subject of *please* and in the second the object. This would be indicated by providing a deep structure for the second sentence of some such form as *It is easy to please John.*

One obvious counter-example to the claim that deep structures contain all the information necessary for semantic interpretation would be transformations which change meaning, such as the optional negative and question transformations given in the 1957 version of Chomsky's theory. The point is that, if these were left as optional transformations which could be applied to any appropriate deep structure, vital semantic information would be missing from the deep structure itself. A meaning assigned to the deep structure of *The dog chases the cat* would be radically altered if an optional negative transformation was later applied resulting in *The dog is not chasing the cat*; in this case it would be the surface structure that contains the information necessary for semantic interpretation. This difficulty is neatly dealt with by the inclusion of transformation markers in deep structure which trigger off obligatory transformations, thus allowing the presence of a negative marker in deep structure to be taken into account when arriving at a semantic interpretation for a sentence. The same would hold for other transformations, since interrogative, imperative and other similar markers would also appear in deep structure.

The interesting thing is that, despite the obvious advantages from the point of view of semantic interpretation, linguists are at pains to point out that the inclusion of transformation markers in deep structure can also be justified on purely formal grounds of permitting greater generalization of syntactic rules. To give the flavour of the type of arguments used, I will again take the case of the passive. One feature of verbs that can be used in the passive form is that they can also take adverbs of manner. For instance, of the two senses of the verb *weigh* in:

John weighs the baby (*carefully*)
John weighs 12 stone

only the first can both take adverbs of manner and be turned into the corresponding passive, i.e., *The baby is weighed* (*carefully*) *by John* but not *12 stone are weighed by John*. In order to express this generalization the apparently bizarre suggestion is made that the deep structure of the passive should take the form of Figure 4. This would allow the *adverb manner* constituent to be rewritten either as a manner adverbial, or as a

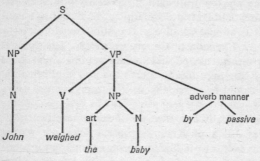

Figure 4

passive marker, or both. This allows the expression of two rules for one: the restrictions concerning which verbs can be used in the passive and the rule about which verbs can take manner adverbs. Similar rationales are applicable to other transformations. But, impressive as these arguments are, for the psychologist the main interest in the change from optional transformations to obligatory transformations marked in deep structure lies in the requirement that all information necessary for semantic interpretation must be included in deep structure.

Turning to surface structure, opposite considerations hold. Since surface structure underlies the phonetic representation of the physical sounds of a sentence, the surface structure of a sentence must consist of linguistic elements in their final derived order after all transformational additions, deletions and permutations have been carried out. The crucial distinction between deep structure and surface structure, then, is that the former specifies the structure of a sentence in such a way as to bring out underlying syntactic relationships, even though this may result in an abstract representation of constituent strings that is far removed from the final form of the sentence. An example would be a sentence such as *The small girl was bitten by the brown dog*, the deep structure of which would be broken up into the following strings: *The dog is brown*, *The dog bit the girl*, *The girl is small*, plus *passive marker*. Surface structure, on the other hand, would have to preserve the ordering of the words in the final sentence so that their phonetic sounds would occur in correct left-to-right sequence. The contention that the transformations needed to achieve this final ordering often result in a distortion of underlying syntactic relations has far reaching implications for theories of how language users produce and understand sentences.

The lexicon

Although in *Aspects of the Theory of Syntax* the lexicon is included in the base of the syntactic component, it is justifiable to discuss it in a separate section, on the grounds of its obvious semantic implications. As this dual aspect has been responsible for a good deal of confusion, the concept of a lexicon will first be introduced in a strictly syntactic context before going on to discuss its status in the grammatical system as a whole.

As mentioned on page 52 the base rules of the 1965 syntactic component include both a set of phrase structure rewriting rules and a lexicon. This brings about a separation of two operations which were combined in the 1957 phrase structure rules. These included rules for rewriting both symbols into other symbols and also symbols into actual words (see, for example, Rules 7 to 10 on page 35).

The difficulty about introducing lexical items by individual rewriting rules of this kind is that there is no way to indicate the restrictions on the choice of words necessary to prevent the generation of deviant sentences. There are basically two kinds of selection restrictions involved. One case is when the syntactic structure of a string limits the selection of possible words. Thus, the rewriting of V as a particular verb depends on whether the syntactic frame requires a transitive or an intransitive verb. One way of dealing with this would be to list all words in a lexicon which assigns features indicating the syntactic contexts in which words can occur. For example, all transitive verbs might have the feature (. . . . NP) which would indicate that only verbs with this contextual feature can appear in this position, i.e. in a sentence with a direct object. A more limited set of verbs such as *say*, *believe* and *hope* might be assigned the feature (. . . . that + S), indicating that they can occur in a sentence frame such as *He believes that life is good*. Chomsky calls features of this kind *strict subcategorization features* because they categorize major word classes, such as nouns and verbs, into sub-classes according to the syntactic frames in which they can occur.

Another kind of selection restriction is concerned with choice of words in relation to the other words occurring in the string. Lack of such restrictions would result in sentences like *John frightens sincerity*, the deviance of which lies in the fact that *frightens* normally occurs with an animate object. Chomsky argues that the most economical way of preventing this is to include in the lexicon features of nouns such as count or mass, animate or inanimate, human or nonhuman, male or female, and so on. Other parts of speech like verbs and adjectives would be assigned contextual features indicating the features of the nouns with which they can occur. For example, *John* would be assigned the features: (N, +animate, +human, +male, etc.) and *sincerity*, (N, +abstract, etc.). The verb *frighten* would have the features: (V, (. . . . NP), (+abstract . . . . +animate), (+animate . . . . +animate, etc.), indicating that *frighten* is a verb, a transitive verb, and that it can occur with either an abstract subject and an animate object or with an animate subject and an animate object. This would allow the selection of *Sincerity frightens John* and *John frightens the man*, but not *John frightens sincerity*. Chomsky calls these latter features *selectional features* because they define the contexts in which a word can be selected in terms of the lexical features of the other words which appear in the string. The same sort of contextual restrictions can be applied to adjectives to prevent such deviant combinations as *The silent banana*.

According to the 1965 system, the rewriting rules, instead of directly generating words, produce preterminal strings into which particular words from the lexicon can be inserted. This would take place according to a general lexical rule stating that only words with appropriate contextual features are candidates for insertion. It should be noted that, since these insertion operations take into account the structure of the string into which the words are inserted, they are technically transformational rules. In other words, the contextual restrictions are specified in terms of how other symbols are rewritten in the generation of the string.

Chomsky suggests that the distinction between strict subcategorization rules and selectional rules has interesting implications for defining degrees of grammaticalness. He claims that breaking a strict subcategorization rule leads to graver deviations from grammaticalness, since it involves using, say, an intransitive or a transitive verb in the wrong syntactic framework. Breaking selectional rules about which words can co-occur with each other only results in such possibly metaphorical sentences as *That boy frightens sincerity* or *Silent as a banana*.

However, as Chomsky points out, formulation of selection restrictions on choice of words immediately raises the question as to whether one is dealing with syntactic or semantic constraints. Taking Chomsky's original example of a syntactically correct but meaningless sentence *Colourless green ideas sleep furiously*, this would now be classified as ungrammatical at the selectional rule level, since *sleep* presumably requires an animate subject while *green* can only apply to physical objects. The point at issue is whether the syntactic rules should be allowed to generate such sentences as syntactically permissible; and leave it to the semantic component to reveal the anomalies involved in selecting an incongruous juxtaposition of nouns, verbs and adjectives. Clearly, this is an area of great complexity and in *Aspects of the Theory of Syntax* Chomsky concludes that the question of how these borderline selectional rules should be apportioned between the syntactic and semantic components is still open.

However, the argument about whether the selectional rules should appear in the syntactic component or the semantic component does not affect the basic case for including features such as count/mass, animate/inanimate, human/nonhuman, male/female in the lexicon. For one thing, many apparently semantic features are involved in rules that are clearly syntactic. For example, *The chair whom I sat on* and *John cut herself* are ungrammatical by any standard.

More importantly, the role of the lexicon in the grammatical system is much broader than that of preventing generation of deviant strings. As Chomsky puts it in *Topics in the Theory of Generative Grammar*, the lexicon should contain all the information that is idiosyncratic to a particular lexical item. This includes not only contextual features of the kind discussed above but also semantic and phonological features. In fact, rather than thinking of items in the lexicon as words, a more accurate conception would be that each lexical item is a bundle of features. These would include a phonetic representation of its constituent sounds, and clusters of syntactic and semantic features; in other words everything about a word that is relevant to its use in the language.

The crucial point to grasp is that there is no basic contradiction between the inclusion of semantic and phonological features in the lexicon and its position in the base of the syntactic component. As shown in Figure 3 the syntactic component provides the input to the semantic and phonological components. Under the system envisaged in the 1965 theory, the phrase structure rules of the base generate a hierarchical tree diagram providing slots into which items from the lexicon can be inserted. Some lexical features will be directly relevant to deciding whether an individual item can be inserted into that particular framework. If an item *is* acceptable, the whole cluster of features assigned to that word will be inserted. This means that the output to the semantic component will take the form of a deep structure framework plus all the semantic features associated with the lexical items. This, of course, is just the syntactic and lexical information required for semantic interpretation. Output to the phonological component will be the surface structure (after all transformations have been carried out) plus the phonological features from the lexicon needed to arrive at a phonetic representation of the sounds of the sentence. The basic notion is that the lexicon provides a pool of lexical information about words which can be channelled appropriately to every part of the system.

However, as will be seen in the next section, the idea of a semantic component was first introduced in slightly different terms which gave an impression of overlap as regards both lexical features and selectional rules.

Semantic component: Katz and Fodor's theory

In order to get clear the status of the semantic component in the 1965 version of Chomsky's theory, it is helpful to know how this new element came to be introduced into the grammar. During the period between 1957 and 1965 a classic article by Katz and Fodor proposing a semantic theory appeared in the journal *Language* (1963). It is this theory that was incorporated into Chomsky's system as the rules of the semantic component.

Katz and Fodor's theory was designed to perform two functions: first, to provide a systematic basis for picking out synonymous, ambiguous and anomalous sentences and, secondly, to assign semantic interpretations to permissible sentences. They started off from the position that some features of sentences can be accounted for only in terms of lexical meaning. For instance, the ambiguity of a sentence like *The bill is large* cannot be explained by any syntactical differences but is due to the two possible meanings of the word *bill*. This means that a full account of a language will have to include a systematic listing of all the possible meanings of individual words, an aspect that was not catered for in Chomsky's earlier 1957 theory.

However, Katz and Fodor also recognized that in order to

understand a sentence it is necessary to know not only the meanings of individual words but also the syntactic relations between them. Consequently, their semantic rules were designed to apply to sentences whose syntactic structures were already given in the form of phrase structure tree diagrams. It was not made clear, originally, whether these represented the deep structure or the surface form of a sentence. When the distinction between deep and surface structure was emphasized in the 1965 version of transformational grammar, a main justification for deep structure was that meaning relations between sentences are manifest only at this level. As a result, deep structure phrase markers were proposed as the input to the semantic component, which by this time was thought to consist of rules of the type suggested by Katz and Fodor. However, as the examples given in the Katz and Fodor article refer to simple sentences (for which there is a minimum difference between deep and surface tree diagrams), their proposals are not vitiated by the later distinction between deep and surface structure.

The first problem facing a theory that tries to account for the combination of individual word meanings into whole sentences is how to characterize word meanings in such a way that systematic relations between them can be expressed. If each word, or sense of a word, has a unique dictionary definition, then individual rules would be necessary for specifying the combination of each pair of words. Katz and Fodor hit upon the idea of breaking down the total definitions of words into what might be called 'atoms of meaning'. These atoms, or *semantic markers* as they were called, are systematic throughout the dictionary in the sense that they are used to define distinctions of meaning between whole sets of words. Examples of semantic markers would be human/nonhuman, male/female, and so on. The latter, for instance, expresses the relation between a whole series of word pairs such as man and woman, bull and cow, bachelor and spinster, uncle and aunt, and so on. The idea is that such pairs would have identical meanings if this distinguishing 'sex' marker did not exist.

An example of a dictionary entry taken from Katz and

Fodor is shown in Figure 5, in which each branch of markers represents a different sense of the word *bachelor*. Starting from the top, the first syntactic marker 'noun' indicates that only those senses of a word classified as nouns are being considered. This would obviously be an important distinction for many words such as *run*, *dog*, *chase* and even *cat*. In round brackets are the semantic markers which represent the meanings of the word in terms which are used systematically to define many words in the dictionary. In square brackets are semantic distinguishers, the point about them being that they are supposed to distinguish only between senses of the one word *bachelor* and are therefore idiosyncratic to that word.

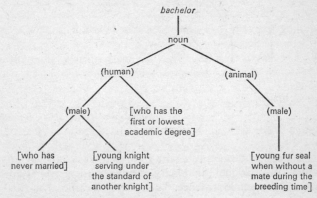

Figure 5 (From Katz and Fodor, 1963)

Katz and Fodor suggest that some of the meanings in the distinguishers could be reanalysed as semantic markers because they make more general distinctions: in the *bachelor* diagram 'young' could appear as a semantic marker for the second and fourth senses of the word. Later critics have argued that by continuing this process the whole class of distinguishers would become obsolete, since they can all be broken down into elements which have wider meanings. This would simplify the theory conceptually but at the expense of greatly increasing the number of semantic markers. However, as the total number of markers is certain to be enormous in any case, it seems a perfectly reasonable step. One method that Katz and Fodor suggest for cutting down the number of markers that have to appear in each dictionary entry is to include redundancy rules indicating that some markers automatically entail certain higher order markers. For instance, the marker 'human' implies that the word also has the markers animal, physical object, solid, organic, and so on.

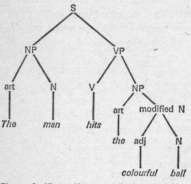

Figure 6 (From Katz and Fodor, 1963)

The next problem is to devise rules that govern the combination of individual dictionary meanings to arrive at the meaning of a whole sentence. As emphasized earlier, Katz and Fodor's system depends on the syntactic structure of a sentence being given. For instance, for the sentence in Figure 6, it is essential to know that *colourful* modifies *ball* rather than *man*, that *the colourful ball* is the direct object of the verb *hits* and that *The man* is the subject of the whole sentence. The rules for semantic interpretation, called *projection rules* by Katz and Fodor, state that words occurring together in units at the lowest level of the tree diagram must be combined first. Then the process can proceed up the tree combining larger and larger units until the meaning of the whole sentence is arrived at. In Figure 6 this would mean that either *The* and *man* or *colourful* and *ball* could be combined as a first step, but not *man* and *hits* or *hits* and *the*, which cut across the constituent units of the sentence.

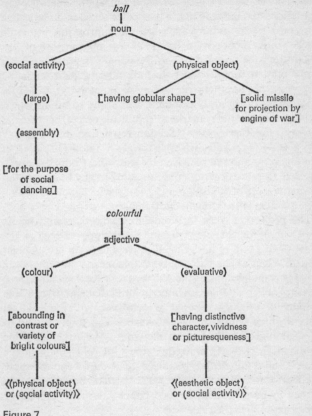

Figure 7

The actual rules for making these combinations depend on the notion of selection restrictions. To show how these work, the dictionary entries for *colourful* and *ball* are given in Figure 7. The selection restrictions shown in angle brackets at the end of the branches for *colourful* indicate which senses of the word can apply to which types of nouns. It is at this point that one sees the crucial importance of the atomization of meaning into semantic markers. Instead of having to give a list of all the individual nouns to which *colourful* can apply, the selection restrictions can indicate that a particular sense of an adjective can apply to any noun which has the appropriate semantic marker in its dictionary entry. Thus, for the purpose of this illustration, the sense of *colourful* meaning 'picturesque' can apply only to nouns which include among their semantic markers either (aesthetic object) or (social activity). *Colourful* in the sense of 'brightly coloured' can apply to nouns which include among their markers (physical object) or (social activity). In other cases a selection restriction might specify that a sense of an adjective applies only if a noun has both of two markers; an example given by Katz and Fodor is *honest*, which in its more general sense can apply to any human noun, but in the sense of 'chaste' only to nouns which include among their markers both (human) *and* (female).

The projection rules for combining adjectives and nouns state that, as long as these selection restrictions are met, all the semantic markers of both the adjective and noun are amalgamated. When applied to Figure 7 this means that of the six possible combinations of the two senses of *colourful* and three senses of *ball*, only four can undergo this amalgamation. These include the 'brightly coloured' sense of *colourful* which can go with all three senses of *ball* because it can apply either to physical objects or to social activities. The other possible combination is the 'picturesque' sense of *colourful* with the 'dance' sense of *ball*; but this sense of *colourful* cannot apply to either of the physical object senses of *ball* because it only applies to nouns which include either (aesthetic object) or (social activity) in their markers.

Referring back to Figure 6, the next step would be to add *the* in the sense of 'some definite' to all four combinations for *colourful ball*. Next comes the amalgamation of the verb *hits*. Selection restrictions for verbs are given in the form of permissible subjects and objects. For their example, Katz and Fodor distinguish two senses of *hits*: 'collide with', in which case both subject and object can be any physical object, and 'strike with hand or instrument', in which case the object can still be any physical object but the subject must be human or at least higher animal. Combining *hits* and *the colourful ball* would thus result in eliminating the two senses of *colourful ball* which concern a 'brightly coloured' or 'picturesque' dance, since there is no marker for (physical object) in these amalgamations as required for the direct object of *hits*. However, *man* can be combined as subject with both senses of *hits* since its markers would include both (physical object) and (higher animal). This leaves one with a grand total of four amalgamations of semantic markers representing four possible meanings of the sentence. These could roughly be translated as 'Some definite human adult male collides with (or strikes) some definite brightly coloured globular shape (or war missile)'.

This example gives an indication of the type of projection or amalgamation rules proposed by the theory. The important point is that they provide a set of systematic rules for joining up meanings of individual words in a way determined by the overall syntactic structure of the sentence. This means that for any given sentence the number of ambiguous semantic readings will depend both on the number of possible deep structures a sentence may have and the number of possible amalgamations of word meanings for each of these structures. In this way both syntactic and lexical ambiguity are dealt with.

It should be immediately apparent that there are great similarities between some of Katz and Fodor's semantic markers and the features proposed by Chomsky for the lexicon. Moreover, in both cases it can be argued that a hierarchical structure is not the best way of representing such distinctions. It is true that some semantic markers are hierarchical, as is shown by the redundancy rules mentioned above which depend on the fact that a marker such as physical object is in some sense prior to, and entailed by, the division into human or non-human. However, there is no reason why the human/non-human distinction should come before or after the male/female distinction. If one divides all animals into male or female, as in the left half of Figure 8, then one has to repeat the human or non-human division under both the male and female branches.

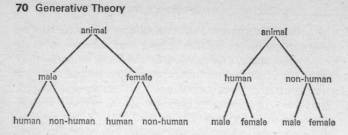

Figure 8

Alternatively, a prior division into human or non-human requires a duplication of the male and female markers as in the right half of Figure 8. What it comes down to is that a lexical item can be male or female independently of whether it is human or non-human. This is exactly parallel to the position with many of the features discussed by Chomsky. One example he gives is that nouns can be proper or common independently of whether they are human or non-human (compare *John*, *Egypt*, *boy*, *book*). It was for this reason that Chomsky formulated lexical entries not as hierarchies but as sets of features which could be marked as positive or negative for each lexical item. Thus, *John* would be (+Proper, +Human), *Egypt* (+Proper, −Human), *boy* (−Proper, +Human) and *book* (−Proper, −Human).

Based on similar arguments, a better formulation for Katz and Fodor's dictionary items might be in terms of plus or minus features rather than as tree diagrams of the form shown in figures 5 and 7. In this way the problem of hierarchical ordering of semantic markers could be avoided. It should be noted, however, that this would require separate lexical entries for each sense of a word. Thus, one entry for *bachelor* might be (+human, +male, +who has never married), while other senses would be allotted different sets of semantic features.

If this suggestion were adopted it would obviously pave the way for Katz and Fodor's semantic markers to be included as semantic features in the lexicon. On general grounds of economy it seems preferable to group all lexical information together rather than having a lexicon in the syntactic component and a separate dictionary in the semantic component. Another advantage is that features which are relevant to both syntactic and semantic rules, such as human/non-human and male/female, will have only to be stated once in the lexicon.

Similar considerations apply to the formulation of selection restrictions. Using Chomsky's notation for expressing selectional features by indicating the frames in which words can occur, abbreviated lexicon entries for the word *colourful* might be as follows:

colourful (sense 1): + adj, + (colour), + (. . . . physical object), + (. . . . social activity)
colourful (sense 2): + adj, + (evaluative), + (. . . . aesthetic object), + (. . . . social activity)

This is exactly equivalent to the selection restrictions in angle brackets at the end of the branches of *colourful* in Figure 7, indicating what types of nouns the various senses of *colourful* can be applied to. Entries for the verb *hit* might be as follows:

hit (sense 1): + V, + (collide with), + (physical object . . . . physical object)

hit (sense 2): + V, + (strike), + (higher animal . . . . physical object).

This expresses the restriction that, while *hit* in the first sense can have any physical object as subject or object, *hit* in the second sense can only have a higher animal as subject. Formulated in this way it is clear that these restrictions are exactly the same as the selectional features proposed by Chomsky, and so could also be included in the lexicon.

Since both the syntactic and semantic components can make use of information in the lexicon, this still leaves open the question of whether the selectional rules should appear in the syntactic component, so as to prevent the generation of anomalous sentences in the first place, or in the semantic component, in which case these sentences would be eliminated at a later stage. One argument in favour of the latter solution is that it might be easier to build into the semantic component rules allowing for the metaphorical use of sentences like *John frightens sincerity* or *Colourless green ideas sleep furiously* in poetic or other usage when normal restrictions do not apply.

To sum up, the relation between Katz and Fodor's semantic theory and Chomsky's transformational grammar suggested here is that the dictionary element of Katz and Fodor's theory should be incorporated into the lexicon in the base of the syntactic component. The base rules would then be able to generate deep structures and insert all necessary lexical information in the form of semantic features (i.e. semantic markers). This would form the input to the semantic component which would consist of Katz and Fodor's projection rules for combining the markers of individual words in order to produce semantic interpretations for sentences.

It should be noted that this does not involve any substantive change in Katz and Fodor's theory. Their system is a two stage one, first looking up the words of a sentence in the dictionary and only then bringing into operation the projection rules for combining word meanings. The difference is simply that the first step of looking up the semantic markers of lexical items would now be carried out by reference to the lexicon in the base of the syntactic component. Only the second step of using projection rules to arrive at semantic readings for sentences would be carried out by the semantic component. This fits in exactly with the role of the lexicon proposed in the previous section, the status of the semantic component being purely interpretative of the syntactic and lexical information provided by the syntactic component.

One point that may already have occurred to the reader is that, while it may be true that the semantic readings given for *The man hits the colourful ball* are all theoretically possible, in the first place some of them are more inherently probable than others, and in any case the situation in which they are uttered will very often make it clear which meaning is intended. These facts depend on the language user's knowledge of the world, and Katz and Fodor, and many other semantic theorists, would claim that a semantic theory cannot be expected to deal with this aspect of meaning. The argument is that, otherwise, the whole attempt would have to be abandoned since it would be necessary to describe the language user's entire knowledge of the world and also his complete socio-physical context at the time of an utterance. For example, the probable anomaly of saying *Mr Heath, leader of the Labour Party, spoke in favour of nationalization* is obvious only to someone knowing current party political alignments. Katz and Fodor want to limit their account to those semantic facts which would be known by any speaker of English regardless of his knowledge of current affairs.

At first sight this seems a perfectly reasonable distinction. The semantic component can be thought of as describing the language user's ability to understand all possible semantic readings of a sentence in the same way as the syntactic component gives the rules for producing all possible grammatical sentences. Which particular sentence is uttered or which interpretation is accepted on any one occasion is a matter beyond the scope of a purely linguistic theory.

The real difficulty arises because it can plausibly be argued that semantic markers are themselves based on knowledge of the world; for instance, the knowledge that cats and dogs are animals but not human (except perhaps in their owners' eyes). Moreover, some markers seem to depend merely on current conventions. A nice example is the allocation of the marker (male) to the word *priest*, which would mean that the sentence *The landlord knocked up the priest* could be given only the interpretation 'The landlord awakened the priest by knocking on his door'. Clearly, the possibility of women being ordained would allow another interpretation. At present there appears to be no generally satisfactory solution to this problem of making a distinction between knowledge of a language and knowledge of the world.

Even leaving this difficulty on one side, the attempt to enumerate full sets of semantic markers for words has presented many problems. Allocation of markers has been governed by two criteria. The first is the need to provide markers that will distinguish between the meanings of otherwise similar words, as represented, for instance, by the difficulty of devising markers to make a distinction between *apple* and *pear* or *lend* and *borrow*. The other criterion is that markers are required to account for a native speaker's awareness of disambiguating and anomalous sentences. Examples of disambiguating sentences taken from a critique by Bolinger (1965) of Katz and Fodor's theory are *He became a bachelor* and *That peasant is a happy bachelor*. The fact that we know that the first sentence cannot refer to 'never having been married' means, Bolinger argues, that there must be some sort of 'not possible to become' marker in that sense of the word. Equally elimination of the 'knight' sense in the sentence about the peasant implies that there must be a marker for 'noble' in that branch. Similarly, in order to prevent anomalous sentences such as *The apple is square* and *The apple is blue*, shape and colour markers have to be added to the features of nouns (with the extra difficulty of explaining why if one did say *The apple is blue* one would mean that it had been artificially coloured in some way). Applying these same requirements to sets of adjectives indicating shape, height, length, etc., and to verbs such as *have*, *give*, *lend*, *steal*, have proved formidable tasks. Again with these examples it will be seen how difficult it is to draw the line between linguistic and 'real life' knowledge.

Nevertheless, in spite of all the difficulties, Katz and Fodor's basic idea of breaking down word meanings into semantic markers or features opened up for the first time the possibility of a systematic theory of meaning taking into account both lexical and syntactic information.

Phonological component

In this section, rather than going into the technicalities of phonetic transcription, I shall concentrate on those aspects of the phonological component which have implications for the grammar as a whole. As explained earlier, it is the surface structures of sentences which form the input to the phonological component. The reason for this is that the surface structure is the result of rearrangements carried out by transformational rules to convert the elements in deep structure into the final ordering that underlies the spoken sentence. To take just one example, the surface structure of a passive like *Jane is chased by John* will indicate that the logical object of the deep structure Jane has been transferred to the front of the sentence to function as its surface grammatical subject, while the agentive phrase *by* plus underlying logical subject *John* has been placed at the end.

In *Syntactic Structures* the morphophonemical rules were thought of as converting the morphemes in a terminal string into phonemes (the technical linguistic meanings of these terms are given on pages 44ff). The main difference between the 1957 and 1965 versions is that during this period Chomsky, in collaboration with Morris Halle (Chomsky and Halle 1968), had developed the theory of distinctive features suggested by the distinguished linguist Roman Jakobson. This involves characterizing sounds in terms of a set of binary articulatory features such as voiced or voiceless, nasal or non-nasal, and so on. The idea is that any sound can be fully represented by assigning it plus or minus features on these binary dimensions. Chomsky suggests that each item in the lexicon, which are strictly morphemes rather than words, should be allocated a sequence of such phonological feature sets indicating the consecutive sounds making up the morpheme (as in *c–a–t*). These entries represent the underlying 'absolute' phonological form of the morpheme. But when put together in a sentence, the sounds of morphemes change according to the context in which they occur. For instance, the sounds of many verbs are quite different as a function of the tense or number morphemes with which they are associated. Examples are *take* versus *took*, *go* versus *went*, while the form of the indefinite article appears as *a* or *an* as a function of the letter beginning the next word. Using the information given in the lexicon, including idiosyncratic irregularities, it is the function of the phonological rules to apply a series of cyclical transformations to make these contextual adjustments. These operate by starting with the most deeply embedded units and working upwards through the surface structure of the sentence, in just the same way that the semantic rules carry out amalgamations proceeding from the lowest to the highest level units in deep structure. The end product of the phonological rules is what Chomsky calls a phonetic representation, giving a derived sequence of phonological features which represent the actual spoken sounds of the sentence.

For technical reasons I will not go into here, Chomsky argues that there is no intermediate stage between the absolute phonological representation of morphemes, which forms the input to the phonological component, and the phonetic representation of actual sounds. This leads him to deny the independent existence of the phoneme, since there is no level of phonemic representation involved in the working of the phonological rules. It should be noted, however, that the phoneme is still accepted as a basic linguistic unit by many linguists.

From a psychological point of view, the chief point of interest about Chomsky's formulation of the phonological component is the way in which it provides a mirror image of the semantic component. Both are interpretative in that they operate on the output of the syntactic component, in the case of the phonological component on the surface structure and in the case of the semantic component on the deep structure. It has been pointed out that this lack of any direct link between the semantic and phonological components explains the essential arbitrariness of the connection between the sound, or form, of a word and its meaning.

Another similarity is that both phonological and semantic representations are expressed in terms of plus or minus features. In fact, it was probably the development of binary distinctive features in phonology which stimulated the idea of extending the same system to semantics and syntax. The aim is to arrive at a universal set of features which will include all the possible phonological, semantic and syntactic features that appear in natural languages, although the selection of particular features will vary from language to language. It is generally recognized that a universal alphabet of phonetic features is desirable and considerable progress has been made towards compiling one. Providing lists of universal syntactic and semantic features is a more problematical task. Nevertheless, the final objective is to incorporate phonological, syntactic and semantic universals into a general theory of the form of language, which will provide an explanatory basis for their realizations in the grammars of particular languages.

Comparison with 1957 theory

Probably the most useful summary of the 1965 version of Chomsky's theory is in terms of the similarities and differences between it and the 1957 version. One of the most obvious differences is the change from the earlier emphasis on a division between 'kernel' sentences, defined as those which require only obligatory transformations, and more complex sentences, which are formed by optional transformations operating on one or more underlying strings. In the 1965 version more attention is given to the fact that all sentences have a deep structure and a surface structure. Further, the transformations which map deep on to surface structures have all become obligatory, since the surface form of the sentence is fully determined by the deep structure, which includes all the constituent strings which will be combined to produce the final sentence.

However, in spite of the differences in terminology, this shift in emphasis formalizes a distinction that was implicit in the earlier version. In the 1957 theory the introduction of transformations was justified on the grounds that they were needed to account for syntactic ambiguities. Examples are sentences such as *The shooting of the hunters was awful* and *Visiting relatives can be a nuisance*, for which it can be shown that the different interpretations are transformationally derived from different underlying kernel strings. In the terminology of the 1965 version this is equivalent to saying that such sentences have one surface structure but two or more deep structures. Equally, in the later version 'kernel' sentences are still those which require only a few transformations to arrive at their surface form, or in other words their deep and surface structures are similar because a minimal number of transformational changes have been introduced. The difficulty is that, with the abolition of the distinction between obligatory and optional transformations, there is no precise way of formulating this.

The other major innovations in the 1965 theory were the semantic component and the lexicon. As explained earlier, these were developed in parallel so that some of the functions of Chomsky's lexicon and Katz and Fodor's semantic theory overlap. The essential point is that it is deep structure which provides the information about basic grammatical relations needed for semantic interpretation. It is in this connection that the specification of all transformations as obligatory in deep structure is important, since some of the original optional transformations (e.g. the negative and interrogative) bring about meaning changes that can only be taken into account by the semantic component if they are marked in deep structure.

This syntactic information obviously has to be supplemented by lexical information about the possible meanings of individual words. Katz and Fodor proposed a dictionary containing definitions of words in terms of semantic markers. It was later suggested that these markers could be incorporated as semantic features into the lexicon which forms part of the base syntactic component. This means that, unlike the 1957 version, in which words were introduced into terminal strings at the final stage of the phrase structure rewriting rules, the 1965 system separates these two operations. The phrase structure rewriting rules produce a grammatical framework into which words from the lexicon can be inserted with all their semantic and phonological features. The output of the syntactic component to the semantic component takes the form of this deep structure plus the semantic features of constituent words, thus providing all the syntactic and lexical information required for semantic interpretation. The output to the phonological component consists of the surface structure plus the phonological features of the words, thus providing all the syntactic and phonological information needed to arrive at a phonetic representation of the actual sounds of the sentence. In this way the syntactic component acts as the generative source in the system producing all the information about a sentence necessary to account for its form and meaning (as shown in Figure 3).

One final point, which applies to both the 1957 and 1965 versions of the theory, is a possible confusion that might arise from the fact that much of Chomsky's writing is aimed at demonstrating the inadequacy of phrase structure grammars as compared with transformational grammar. It may seem decidedly puzzling, therefore, that the fundamental role of generating underlying deep structures is carried out by a set of phrase structure rewriting rules. The crucial difference is that the theories Chomsky is attacking are those which maintain that a phrase structure, or immediate constituent, analysis of the *surface* form of a sentence is all that is required for an adequate grammatical analysis. Chomsky's opposition to this is based on two main arguments. First, he demonstrates that it would be extremely uneconomic, if not impossible, to generate all surface structures directly. Secondly, he argues that an immediate constituent analysis of surface structure provides only the kind of structural information necessary for phonological representation. In order to carry out a full grammatical analysis it is necessary to follow through the series of transformations linking surface form to deep structure, since it is only the latter that represents the basic grammatical relations needed for semantic interpretation.

But, while the proposed transformational link between the two structural levels is clear enough, some confusion enters as to how the deep and surface structures of sentences are to be represented. In *Topics in the Theory of Generative Grammar* Chomsky says that surface structure consists of a labelled bracketing, or tree diagram, of a sentence. This would be equivalent to an immediate constituent analysis. Chomsky goes on to make the point that deep structure must be different from this since it indicates underlying grammatical relations that are not revealed in surface structure. However, since deep structures are generated by phrase structure rules, they too can be represented by a labelled tree diagram showing the branching resulting from the operation of rewriting rules. And for simple 'kernel' sentences the simplified tree diagrams often given as examples would in fact look very similar. An example would be the sentence shown in Figure 6, where what amounts to an immediate constituent analysis of the sentence also represents its underlying phrase structure. This is due to the minimal amount of transformational distortion. But for more complex sentences deep structure and surface structure tree diagrams would be very different, involving, for instance, in the case of the passive a change of grammatical subject. The fact that in many cases both deep structure and surface structure appear to be arrived at in practice by a similar sort of phrase structure analysis should not obscure their difference in status, surface structure being derived as a result of applying transformations to deep structure. In a fully worked out transformational grammar representation of surface structure would be dependent on the effect of such transformations rather than on an analysis of surface constituents. I have gone into this point at some length because much psychological research investigating the effect of syntactic structures makes use of tree diagrams, and it is important to know whether they are meant to portray deep or surface structure.

Evaluation

As far as the requirements of the three levels of adequacy described on page 34 are concerned, the 1965 version of Chomsky's theory meets them for the same reasons as the 1957 version, due to the fundamental similarities between the two versions. Their weak generative power is theoretically equivalent. In the 1957 theory the capacity to generate an infinite number of sentences was catered for by the generalized transformations which could combine an unlimited number of individual 'kernel' strings. In the 1965 theory the same role is played by generalized deep structure markers which can contain an unlimited number of constituent sentence strings.

From the point of view of descriptive adequacy, defined as the capacity to generate structural descriptions that accord with native speakers' intuitions, this has been a constant motivation for development of the theory. As has been stressed, the concepts of deep and surface structure arose out of the fact that much of what the native speaker understands about sentences cannot be explained in terms of surface structure but depends on an awareness of underlying grammatical relations expressed in deep structure. In *Syntactic Structures* there is a slight sense of uneasiness about relying on people's understanding of meaning relations between sentences because this appears to smack of semantic considerations. But this is regularized by the introduction of the semantic component in the 1965 version where it is clearly acknowledged that it is the job of the syntactic component to provide a structural description giving all the information necessary for semantic interpretation. Further, the basis for judging the adequacy of a gram-mar in mirroring a native speaker's knowledge of the language is now firmly placed on linguistic intuition. For studying his own language the linguist has available his own intuitions, subject to checking with other native speakers. And, not surprisingly, when attempting to write grammars for other languages the first thing the linguist does is to learn the language himself.

Coming to the third level of explanatory adequacy, the main criterion for evaluating a set of grammatical rules is the degree to which they are capable of expressing underlying generalizations that will account for as many as possible apparent irregularities with the fewest number of *ad hoc* exceptions. The claim is that the idea of deep and surface structure linked by obligatory transformations allows the possibility of expressing many simplifying generalizations about how syntactic rules operate. Similarly, the subdivision of the base rules into rewriting rules and a lexicon makes possible the statement of a general rule for inserting words into appropriate syntactic frames.

One factor that tends to obscure the operation of this economy criterion is that grammars seem to get more and more complicated rather than simpler. The reason for this is that, as the study of language gets more sophisticated, it naturally turns up an increasingly large number of apparent exceptions to the rules so far proposed. For instance, as Chomsky points out, it was not until the attempt was made to provide explicit generative rules that the disadvantages of introducing words into strings by rewriting rules was realized, leading to the necessity for postulating a lexicon. Efforts to specify the form of lexical entries have given rise to a fresh crop of problems. Certainly, the whole point of the exercise is to devise more general rules which will eliminate the need for unrelated *ad hoc* rules to deal with localized sections of the grammar. Nevertheless, depending on the state of the game, it may sometimes appear that increasing complexity arising from the attempt to cope with more aspects of language outweighs the discovery of simplifying generalizations.

A more crucial point is that, as the nature of language becomes more fully understood through the discovery of features universal to all languages, correspondingly fewer rules will need to be stated for individual languages. If it can be demonstrated that all languages have deep and surface structures and that the transformations connecting them can be of a limited type only, such limitations could be included in universal grammar and would not appear in particular grammars. It has further been suggested that the base rules for generating deep structures are themselves universal since they express basic grammatical relations which are found in all languages. If this were so, these rules, and perhaps also the semantic projection rules which operate on deep structures, would not have to appear in individual grammars either. Similarly, if phonological, syntactic and semantic features were universal in the sense that they come from a single universal list, again these would not have to be stated in individual grammars. The only kind of information that would be required for a particular language would be the arbitrary combinations of phonological, syntactic and semantic features appearing in the lexicon, i.e. the vocabulary of the language, plus the particular transformations used to convert universal deep structures into the surface structures idiosyncratic to that language.

To the extent that such a universal grammar can be developed, it obviously has crucial implications not only for linguistic analysis but also, Chomsky argues, for theories of language acquisition and the character of human intelligence. The rationale for explanatory adequacy is that a grammatical theory must be able to account for the way a child learns its native language. In so far as all children develop similar kinds of grammars, these aspects of language are presumed to be universal. In the same way as a linguist equipped with the principles of universal grammar would know what types of rules to look for in some unknown language, so it is suggested that the child is equipped by virtue of the structure of the human brain to develop the appropriate system of rules for learning whatever natural language he happens to be exposed to.

The existence of linguistic universals is still a matter of debate among linguists. For one thing, there is the danger that linguists who believe in them will always find them, because any *differences* between languages will be classified as superficial, and sidetracked by taking the argument down to a more abstract level – perhaps ending up by saying nothing more than that all languages are used to converse about 'things' which act or are acted upon and which are modified by descriptive terms and placed in space and time. Also, it could turn out that when one attempts to write grammars for languages that appear very different from English (Chinese, for example) it might be found that they could be described more economically by different types of rules. Despite these warnings, however, there is no doubt that the hypothesis that there is a universal grammar determining the underlying structure of all languages, and that it contains the structural organization and features proposed by transformational grammar, has proved both challenging and productive.

That this is so is amply demonstrated by the fact that virtually all developments which have taken place since 1965 have been based on Chomsky's conception of what a linguistic theory should aim to achieve. Disagreements have arisen about how to achieve these aims but not about the aims themselves. Leaving aside the numerous syntactic devices that have been suggested to deal with difficulties arising out of attempts to extend the application of transformational grammar, there have been two major developments of interest to psychologists.

The first is a proposal that the basic relations in deep structure are not those between subject and object. These, it is argued, are relatively superficial and may vary from language to language. C. J. Fillmore (1968) suggests that a more revealing analysis of deep structure would be in terms of *cases*, such as agentive, instrumental and dative, since these give a clear indication of word functions in relation to each other. A 'case grammar' of this sort certainly meets the requirement that deep structure should contain all the information needed for semantic analysis in a particularly plausible way. For example, in sentences like *John broke the window* and *A hammer broke the window*, a deep structure analysis which designated *John* as the subject of the first and *A hammer* as the subject of the second would be missing certain relationships that are understood by native speakers. Fillmore would classify *John* in *John broke the window* as agentive but *A hammer* in *A hammer broke the window* as instrumental. This explains why it is possible to say *John broke the window with a hammer* but not *A hammer broke the window with a chisel*. The argument is that the rules governing which of the various cases can be turned into the subject or object of a sentence vary considerably in different languages. Therefore, since the transformations linking deep structure cases to superficial subject and object positions are idiosyncratic to each language, such notions are properly a matter of surface structure. This is an interesting approach which is not incompatible with the spirit of Chomsky's concept of deep and surface structure, as has been pointed out by Chomsky (1971).

The second development aims at a more radical revision of transformational theory. While offering a different analysis of underlying syntactic structure, 'case grammar' accepts the basic position that a prior syntactic analysis is required for semantic interpretation. What supporters of 'generative semantics' propose is that the roles of the syntactic and semantic components should be reversed. There are various different versions but the basic idea is that the generative process should start by producing strings of semantic clusters, specifying the semantic markers of individual words and the semantic relations between them. The syntactic component would thus be relegated to the purely interpretative role of operating on the output of the semantic component. An important argument in favour of this arrangement is that it accounts for similarities between sentences that are not reflected in deep structure. In just the same way that the case for deep structure rests on the fact that similarities between, say, actives and passives are not reflected in surface structure, so it is argued that the similarity between *Harry sold the car to John* and *John bought the car from Harry* can be explained only on the level of a reciprocal relationship between the semantic features of *bought* and *sold*.

The attraction for psychologists of generative semantics is the greater plausibility of supposing that a speaker begins by generating the basic semantic content of 'what he wants to say', only then going on to cast it in an appropriate syntactic form. However, in a recently published article (1971) Chomsky has produced several counter arguments. One of his main points is that any notion of temporal direction of mapping operations involves a total misunderstanding of his theory. The fact that transformational theory postulates a generative syntactic component which initiates the input required for the semantic and phonological components carries no temporal implications about the order in which such operations might be performed by a language user. This line of argument leads to the conclusion that theories which retain all the elements of transformational grammar, while proposing that semantic representations should be generated first and only then mapped on to deep structure, are meaningless in the sense that they are merely restatements of transformational grammar, since the direction of mapping operations is irrelevant.

Chomsky goes on to argue that semantically based grammars which do incorporate the substantial change of replacing deep structures by semantic representations fail to provide all the information about deep structure relations necessary for overall interpretation of a sentence. The generative semanticists, on the other hand, could reply that semantic relations, such as those holding between *sell* and *buy*, and other similar pairs like *present* and *absent*, must be represented at some level of analysis in order to account for the way people understand sentences.

What it comes down to is that, if deep structure by definition contains all the information necessary for semantic interpretation, then some way must be found to express such relationships in deep structure. The difficulty is that deep structure has generally been thought of as expressing underlying relations between actual specific words. As Clark has put it in a recent article (1971), deep structure propositions 'retain all the lexical items of surface structure intact'. This makes it impossible, he argues, for *John is absent* to be represented in some such form as (*false* (*John present*)), which brings out a relationship between *present* and *absent* understood by native speakers.

However, it could equally well be argued that this is an unnecessarily limiting assumption, especially in the light of the abstract nature of deep structure representations, which often contain elements that are deleted or added to in final surface structure. Further, there seems no reason in principle why the semantic features of items inserted into deep structure from the lexicon should not contain information about reciprocal relationships between *sell* and *buy*, *present* and *absent*, and so on. Indeed, some of the latest attempts to devise sets of semantic markers have included just these sort of relationships. The real point at issue is whether deep structure analysis can be extended in this way without losing equally important insights about other structural relations.

As will be seen in the discussion in Part Two about the validity of psychological models based on linguistic descriptions, the argument about the equivalence of semantic representations and deep structures is still continuing. It must be admitted, too, that the possibility of a neat delineation of deep structure as containing all necessary semantic information is not made any easier by Chomsky's (1971) recent proposal that even surface structure may be relevant to some aspects of meaning. Stress, for instance, which is assigned by the phonological component on the basis of the surface order of words in a sentence, may affect the interpretation given to a sentence. Chomsky gives examples in which differential stress, as in the sentences:

Did John give a book to BILL ?
Did John give a BOOK to Bill ?

indicates different presuppositions about the answer that the speaker expects, i.e.:

No, he gave a book to SAM
No, he gave Bill a RECORD

Other examples show that stress on pronouns can alter the possibilities of who they are referring to. Thus, with the sentence:

John hit Bill and then George hit him

if *him* is unstressed it refers to Bill but if stressed refers to John. Surface structure ordering of elements may also be important, as with the placing of the negative in the sentences:

Not many arrows hit the target
Many arrows didn't hit the target

This makes a difference in meaning not reflected in the single deep structure *Not (many arrows hit the target)*. Instead of following the usual argument that whenever a difference in meaning is found it must be shown in deep structure, Chomsky accepts examples such as these as demonstrating that surface structure features can affect meaning. This proposition goes against Chomsky's own 1965 theory that all the information needed for semantic interpretation must be included in deep structure. However, in this recent reformulation Chomsky claims that it is still possible to maintain that it is the grammatical relations represented in deep structure that determine semantic interpretation; although matters such as the focus or topic of a sentence, reference of pronouns and presuppositions may be affected by stress and surface structure order.

This sort of analysis raises all sorts of fascinating questions, including the extension of semantic interpretation to cover such considerations as what the intonational stress of a sentence indicates about the speaker and listener's shared presuppositions about possible responses to a sentence. However, a lot of the discussion hinges on linguists' intuitions about extremely subtle differences in meaning; and, indeed, on their intuitions about what constitutes a 'natural' explanation for complex linguistic phenomena. For the moment, then, it can be said that the case for alternative versions of the relation between semantic representations and syntactic structure remains an open question.

Since these more recent proposals have not been worked through on the same rigorous scale as 'orthodox' transformational grammar, the rest of this book will be mainly concerned with research that has been stimulated by the 1957 and 1965 versions of Chomsky's theory. However, the controversy between the various new schools of thought highlights the dual nature of Chomskyan-influenced linguistics. In support of rival linguistic formulations, linguists base their arguments on the criterion of which offers the best explanation for the native speaker's ability to use and understand language. But this issue has clear psychological implications and is, indeed, central to the whole enterprise of looking to linguistics to provide a basis for psychological models of language, a topic that will be taken up in the introduction to the second part of the book.

Summary

Components of grammar

A grammar consists of three components:

1. *Syntactic component*, comprising *base rules* (equivalent to phrase structure rules in 1957 version but replacing word re-writing rules by lexical rules for inserting words from a lexicon) and *transformational rules* (equivalent to transformational rules in 1957 version). The *lexicon* contains the syntactic, phonological and semantic features of individual words.

2. *Phonological component*, comprising *phonological rules* (equivalent to morphophonemical rules in 1957 version).

3. *Semantic component*, comprising *dictionary entries* for individual words and *projection rules* for combining them according to the syntactic structure of a sentence (no equivalent in 1957 version). It is suggested that the dictionary entries should be incorporated into the lexicon as semantic features.

Definition of deep and surface structure

The syntactic component generates a *deep structure* and a *surface structure* for every sentence. The deep structure is the output of the base rules (basic syntactic relations and lexical semantic features) and the input to the semantic component; the surface structure is the output of the transformational rules (final order of words and lexical phonological features) and the input to the phonological component.

Relation of deep and surface structure to 'kernels'

In the 1965 version all transformations are *obligatory*, being determined by transformation markers in deep structure. The only distinction between 'kernel' and complex sentences lies in the number of obligatory transformations necessary to get from deep to surface structure.

Part Two
Psychological Experiments

4 Rationale for Psycholinguistic Research

Introduction

Before going on to a description of the psychological experiments stimulated by Chomsky's theory, it is important to understand the basic rationale for psycholinguistic research. This rests on the assumption that grammars describe the linguistic competence of the language user. This way of looking at language was a direct result of Chomsky's innovation of expressing grammatical rules in a generative form. Previously, linguists had been concerned mainly with methods for analysing sentences in a given sample of data (as in the technique of immediate constituent analysis described on p. 38). In contrast, Chomsky's requirement that grammatical rules should be able to generate all the sentences in a language seemed to have a direct bearing on the speaker's ability to produce an unlimited number of sentences he has never heard before. This original attraction of Chomsky's theory is brought out in Miller, Galanter and Pribram's book (1960) in which Chomsky's system of generative rules was first put over to psychologists as an analogue of the operations carried out by a speaker when producing a sentence.

However, throughout the brief history of psycholinguistics the question has constantly been raised as to how far it is justified to take linguistic rules as a direct model of language behaviour. As we shall see in the following chapters, the tendency has been to move from models very closely based on transformational grammar to ones that, while drawing on some of the same basic concepts, do not necessarily expect the psychological mechanisms involved to be an exact reflection of linguistic rules. This shift in emphasis has important implications for relations between the two disciplines. On the one hand, the usefulness of basing psychological models on linguistic theory has been increasingly questioned. On the other, there is disagreement about whether linguistic theory should itself be altered in accordance with findings from psychological experiments. The first point is concerned with the degree to which linguistic competence is reflected in performance, an issue that will be taken up in the next section. The second arises from the fact that linguistic analysis is in the last resort based on products of performance, i.e. the potential utterances of native speakers. The validity of linguistic data will form the topic of the third section.

Competence and performance

Attempts to settle the demarcation dispute between linguistics and psychology have centred on a distinction between *competence*, considered the concern of linguistics, and *performance*, considered the concern of psychology. Competence is taken as referring to language in the sense of what constitutes ability to speak a language. Performance, on the other hand, refers to the actual utterances made by language users, the point being that there may not always be an exact correspondence between a speaker's utterances and the linguistic rules of the language.

This separation of the language and the language user operates on several levels. In the first place, actual and potential utterances are all a linguist has to go on when trying to define linguistic competence; it is therefore clearly a problem if speakers' utterances, and even their linguistic intuitions, are not a true reflection of their knowledge of the language. Such lapses can be put down to performance factors such as perceptual and memory limitations but this still leaves the difficulty of deciding which utterances are true indications of the speaker's competence and which are performance deviations.

Another aspect of the competence/performance distinction is a separation between the abstract ability to produce sentences and the choice of a particular utterance on a particular occasion, which may be due to all sorts of situational variables. In this case, investigation into choice of utterances is generally agreed to be on the psychological performance side of the demarcation line, concerned with the motivation of human behaviour rather than with language as such. However, as is brought out in the discussion of speech production models on page 174ff., any such model must allow in principle for the possibility of selecting sentences, even though the motivations for each particular choice may be outside its scope.

But the real problems arise when one comes to look at what is meant by competence itself, as demonstrated by the fact that, in spite of all the performance factors that may be affecting a speaker's utterances, it still makes sense to ask whether he is or is not speaking a particular language. Since this is a question about the speaker's competence, i.e. his ability to speak a language, it would appear to be a matter for analysis by linguists. But the difficulty is that psychologists are also interested in explaining the speaker's ability to use language to convey meanings in a form that can be understood by other speakers of the language. Because both linguists and psychologists are quite legitimately concerned with defining this aspect of competence, the question at issue is to what extent linguistic and psychological accounts of competence coincide. The possibilities of confusion are further confounded by the fact that one can find in Chomsky's writings two glosses given to the definition of competence, one of which has considerably stronger implications for psychology than the other.

One interpretation, which I shall call the weaker, or neutral, definition of competence is that a grammar should provide the best possible *description* of linguistic usage. In Chomsky's terms this would entail a set of rules capable of generating all possible sentences in a language, together with structural descriptions that accord with native speakers' intuitions about grammatical relationships. The implication for psychology is that any psychological model of the language user's behaviour would have to match up to this description of language usage. In other words, by describing what language behaviour involves, linguistic analysis would act as an empirical test for evaluating the output of psychological models.

On the other hand, such an analysis of linguistic competence would have nothing to say about the actual rules or operations by which a language user achieves this output. Equally, of course, no psychological evidence about the operations involved in the production of language would be of relevance to the way in which grammatical rules are formulated. What this amounts to is that there is no necessary connection between the set of rules providing the best descriptive account of a speaker's intuitions and the set of operations by which the speaker himself arrives at these same intuitions.

However, despite this logical distinction, it is very difficult not to slip into the assumption that, if a language user's intuitive knowledge is best described by a set of rules, then these rules must in some way be represented in his mind, even though he may not be consciously aware of them. But this involves a shift from the neutral definition of competence to the stronger interpretation that the rules of grammar are internalized in the head of the speaker and provide the basis for his understanding of linguistic relations. In other words, a step has been taken from a description of *what* the linguistic usage of a native speaker consists of to a hypothesis about *how* he operates when using language.

The conflict between the weaker and stronger interpretations of linguistic competence comes out most clearly when Chomsky moves from the descriptive adequacy of grammatical theories to the concept of explanatory adequacy. Indeed, I shall argue that the root of the ambiguity lies in a discrepancy between the theoretical justification for explanatory adequacy, on the one hand, and the empirical considerations for evaluating it on the other. In practice, the explanatory adequacy of a grammatical theory is judged by its capacity to produce significant generalizations which account for the greatest number of linguistic intuitions. Certainly, this criterion depends on purely linguistic considerations as to what constitutes the best method of analysing linguistic data. There is no necessary implication that these simplifying general rules are the ones actually used by people when producing and understanding sentences.

But the case is very different when it comes to the theoretical justification for explanatory adequacy. This arises from the requirement that a grammatical theory must be able to account for how a child is able to develop a system of grammatical rules that will generate all possible sentences; and, further, how he does this on the basis of the sample of linguistic data to which he happens to be exposed, which will not only be limited but also degenerate in the sense that it will contain many deviant utterances which will somehow have to be rejected from the data. The argument is that, for this to be feasible, the child must have a built-in representation of the principles of universal grammar which constrains his choice of possible sets of grammatical rules. This is not only a hypothesis about how a child learns language. It also implies that during the learning process the grammatical rules of his language are being internalized by the child; and that it is this linguistic competence that underlies the adult's language performance. As Chomsky has written in a recently published article (1970, p. 184), 'A person who has learned a language has acquired a system of rules that relate sound and meaning in a certain specific way. He has, in other words, acquired a certain competence that he puts to use in producing and understanding speech.'

Chomsky goes on to make the claim that, since the ability to learn to speak a natural language is basic to human intelligence, the rules underlying language learning must be characteristic of the way the human mind works. In *Language and Mind* (1968, p. 24) Chomsky writes: 'At the level of universal grammar, [the linguist] is trying to establish certain general properties of human intelligence. Linguistics, so characterized, is simply the sub-field of psychology that deals with these aspects of mind.'

If one accepts this stronger definition that linguistic competence is internalized in the mind of the speaker, what are the implications for the relation between psychology and linguistics? The first point to be made is that the stronger the claims made by linguists about mental processes the more susceptible their theories become to psychological testing. This is because both psychologists and linguists can claim to be making deductions about linguistic operations by looking at relations holding between linguistic input and output. Thus, Chomsky comes to certain conclusions about the kind of grammar a child must be predisposed to look for on the basis of comparing the primary linguistic input to which he is exposed and the final output of adult language. But, equally, if psychological experiments designed to manipulate language input and output show that speakers are using operational rules that in no way resemble the rules of transformational grammar, this has serious implications for the notion that a child learns his language by mastering the generative rules described by transformational theory. And, in so far as the claim is made that the rules of transformational grammar are representative of the way in which the human mind functions, any contrary findings might entail a radical change in the form and organization of the competence hypothesized to underly language use.

However, it must be admitted that when faced with psychological evidence on this issue, Chomsky and his associates have tended to react by retreating to the first more neutral definition of competence, arguing that such evidence is irrelevant to a purely formal analysis of linguistic data. Thus, Chomsky writes in *Aspects of the Theory of Syntax* (1965, p. 9):

When we speak of a grammar as generating a sentence with a certain structural description, we mean simply that the grammar assigns this structural description to the sentence. When we say that a sentence has a certain derivation with respect to a particular generative grammar, we say nothing about how the speaker or hearer might proceed, in some practical or efficient way, to construct such a derivation.

Chomsky treats this as an attempt to clear up a continuing misunderstanding. But in the very same paragraph he describes the aims of generative grammar as being 'to characterise in the most neutral possible terms the knowledge of the language that *provides the basis for actual use of language by a speaker-hearer*' (my italics). He then goes on to say: 'No doubt, a reasonable model of language use will incorporate, as a basic component, the generative grammar that expresses the speaker-hearer's knowledge of the language.' But it is just this claim that 'a person who has learned a language has acquired a system of rules . . . that he puts to use in producing and understanding speech' which needs to be empirically tested. Evidence about psychological mechanisms has no status for proving or disproving a purely descriptive linguistic analysis; but it becomes relevant when such an analysis is used as the basis for a theory of cognitive processes, including the operations underlying speech production and perception. To sum up, there is a distinct tendency among transformational linguists to protect their theories from psychological evidence on the basis of the first, more neutral, definition of competence, while at the same time, under the guise of the stronger definition, making extensive claims about the psychology of cognitive functioning.

This discussion should not, however, be taken to mean that the results of linguistic analysis are not of value to psychologists studying language. The point is that the two definitions of competence have different implications for psychological research. The neutral definition provides a formal analysis of linguistic data, the output of which matches the intuitions of the native speaker. By demonstrating the complexities of the numerous subtle restrictions exhibited in a native speaker's linguistic usage, a grammatical theory acts as a criterion which psychological theories of language have to meet. In this way it prevents over-simplification of the behaviour under study so as to fit in with psychological preconceptions.

The stronger definition of competence has arisen from the irresistible assumption that, if transformational rules provide the 'best' description of the output that a language model must match, they will also provide the 'best' account of the operations speakers use to produce that output. But though it may seem plausible that formal analysis of the potential output of someone who 'knows' a language also represents the speaker's internalized 'knowledge' of the language, this is still a hypothesis. Indeed, it is just this hypothesis that has stimulated new lines of research, turning up factors affecting aspects of language that had never been considered before. Despite

Chomsky's rather aggravating habit of making far-reaching claims about the psychology of human cognition while refusing to acknowledge psychological evidence, as long as the psychologist keeps clear in his mind the difference in status between the definitions of competence, there is no reason why he should not make use of the insights offered by both.

Linguistic data

Up till this point the discussion of the proper relationship between the two disciplines has been concerned with how psychological models can benefit from linguistic theory, the assumption throughout being that grammatical analysis is itself independent of psychological considerations. However, as indicated earlier, the intersection between psychology and linguistics can be looked at the other way round; since grammars are based on native speakers' utterances, or rather their intuitions about possible utterances, psychological investigations of language performance may be of importance in clarifying linguistic data. Some psychologists, notably Broadbent (1970), have criticized Chomsky's theory on the grounds that speakers don't always produce linguistic responses of the form specified by transformational grammar.

There are two main problems here. One is how to extract from the sample of utterances available to the linguist those which are examples of correct sentences, thus rejecting all the many half-finished and other faulty utterances. It is obviously essential to be able to make this distinction if grammars are to be evaluated by their capacity to generate only correct sentences and no incorrect utterances.

The second and even more intractable problem is the requirement that grammars must be able to generate novel sentences which by definition are not present in any given sample. What is needed is extrapolation of a criterion defining the grammaticality of any potential utterance. Chomsky's solution is to rely on native speakers' intuitive knowledge of what constitutes a possible sentence in their own language. But when it comes to investigating these intuitions Chomsky argues against the efficacy of experimental procedures. For one thing, he points out that any such experimental techniques would have to be validated by their success in matching speakers' intuitions in the first place, thus leaving the basic problem untouched.

A further difficulty discussed by Chomsky is that native speakers may not always be consciously aware of their linguistic intuitions. Thus, particularly in an appropriate context, the ambiguity of sentences like *The shooting of the hunters was awful* or *I had a book stolen* may not even be noticed. Nevertheless, Chomsky claims that, once the two possible interpretations are pointed out (usually by means of analogous linguistic examples), the native speaker's intuitive knowledge of the language will lead him to agree that such sentences are transformationally related to two or more different deep structures.

But the main problem in trying to devise experimental procedures to get at these intuitions is to make sure that subjects are making responses on the basis of considerations relevant to linguistic competence. In this connection, Chomsky makes a distinction between acceptability and grammaticalness; judgements about the acceptability of utterances are concerned with performance factors, such as memory limitations and stylistic considerations, which make them clumsy or bizarre to produce and comprehend. He argues that such judgements are irrelevant to the notion of grammaticalness, since many utterances that are not acceptable for one reason or another are perfectly grammatical.

Some of the factors affecting linguistic judgements have been explored in a recent book *Elicitation Experiments in English* by Greenbaum and Quirk (1970). This is devoted to the development of techniques for comparing subjects' judgments about the acceptability of various kinds of verbal material as against their usage elicited and scored under controlled conditions. Some extremely interesting discrepancies were found between judgements and usage; and factors such as the educational background of the subjects and their opinions about the purpose of the tests also affected the responses given. But, though this is undoubtedly a fruitful area for the psychological study of language, the difficulty for the linguist is to disentangle basic grammatical competence from the other variables affecting individual subjects' judgements.

However, despite his pessimism about the likelihood of reliable operational criteria becoming available, Chomsky forcefully makes the point that, at present, the difficulty is not *lack* of reliable evidence but how to account for the mass of linguistic data that would be agreed on by all native speakers. So formidable are the problems involved in devising rules to generate even small sets of unquestionably grammatical sentences that it seems reasonable enough to leave marginal cases of uncertainty and disagreement till a later stage.

In addition, there is the practical consideration that, if no standard usage were accepted, carried to its logical extreme this would mean that a separate grammar would have to be written for each speaker's slightly different usage of the language. Exactly this point is brought out in connection with attempts to write grammars of individual children's linguistic competence. The linguist can then rely neither on his own intuitions about adult language nor on some generally accepted standard of usage among children. In a discussion of this question (1964), Chomsky points out the fallacy of the usual method of basing grammars on recordings of the child's speech utterances, thus ignoring the child's ability to produce novel sentences not in the data. But just because there can be no appeal to 'idealized' native speakers' judgements on the constitution of a potential sentence in one child's language, Chomsky acknowledges the need for 'devious and clever' ways of studying performance in order to get at the child's competence.

Without such procedures there obviously still remains a conceptual difficulty about the criterion for a grammatical sentence, in spite of the practical arguments in favour of relying on linguists' intuitions. Neither occurrence in a limited sample nor a native speaker's untutored judgements are sufficient; so Chomsky defines a grammatical sentence in terms of whether the rules of the grammar will generate a sentence phrase marker for the utterance in question. But this definition is circular; what it comes down to is that sentences that can be generated by the rules of the grammar are counted as grammatical by definition. How, then, can the rules be tested empirically as to whether they generate ungrammatical strings?

The crux of the problem is the attempt of transformational theory to account for the empirical data of natural languages by means of a set of deductive generative rules. In an experimental science like psychology operational criteria of correct responses are laid down in advance by the experimenter. Even the study of operant conditioning in a Skinner box requires an *a priori* decision that any behaviour that results in depressing the lever will count as a correct response, all other behaviour being regarded as non-responses. On the other hand, linguistics is barred from the self-evident criteria applicable in the case of deductive systems of generative rules such as those found in mathematics. It is perfectly permissible to define instances of correct multiplication solely in terms of whether they are generated by the rules for multiplying numbers. This is precisely what is meant by multiplication and there is no question of having to validate the rules against some external behavioural criterion. In this respect, linguistics does indeed seem to be a hard case, balanced in a continual tug of war between the external criterion of matching a speaker's actual performance and the internal criterion of producing a set of generative rules which in themselves define the speaker's potential ability to produce new sentences.

This difficulty is reflected in Chomsky's treatment of the performance variables that intervene between linguistic competence and performance. When he talks about the difference between acceptable and unacceptable sentences being due to performance factors, there seems to be a considerable conceptual difference between systematic memory limitations, which might make it *impossible* for certain sentences ever to be produced, and the kind of fluctuating memory lapses which might result in a sentence being left unfinished on one particular occasion. The point is that, if some extremely complex utterance (such as an embedded sentence instanced by George Miller: *The race that the car that the people whom the obviously not very well dressed man called sold won was held last summer*) could *never* occur in a sample of speech because of fundamental limitations of human information processing (at least without resorting to artificial paper and pencil analysis), to what extent can it be said to form part of even the potential linguistic data of a natural language?

Chomsky claims that it would be impossible to formulate the rules of the grammar in such a way as to exclude such utterances. But this is not self-evident since the rules of transformational grammars are constantly being altered in order to exclude utterances that are accepted as being ungrammatical. What it comes down to is that in one case the linguist's intuition tells him that a distinction between one sentence and another is linguistically significant; in the other the distinction seems arbitrary, as in the above example, imposing a cut-off point on the number of clause embeddings allowed. Indeed, in the recently published Bertrand Russell Memorial Lectures Chomsky (1972) has gone on to argue that such limitations provide no revealing insights into the nature of the human mind just because they are easily explained on 'functional' grounds (such as finite memory capacity), which might apply to any artificial non-human system of information processing. It is only 'formal' operations, which can be shown to be universal to all languages and yet cannot be predicted on general functional grounds, that tell us anything interesting about the properties of the human language-using mind. Fascinating as this line of argument is, the danger is that any data fitting in with a linguist's preconceptions about specifically linguistic universals will be counted as evidence for the basic structure of language, while any awkward data can be put down to the influence of 'functional' performance factors.

To sum up the position on linguistic data in terms of the relations between linguistics and psychology, the main confusion stems from the fact that linguistics can be said to be empirical but not experimental. While this exposes it to obvious criticisms about the criteria used to validate theory against data, it can also be argued that experimental procedures have not been too successful in tapping the abilities involved in people's creative use of natural language.

One final point is that, if valid operational tests for defining linguistic usage were developed, these would have quite different implications for the two definitions of competence. Under the weaker definition all that would be required would be for the rules of transformational grammar to be altered so as to account for the new data. Indeed, the major impetus behind the increasing complexity of grammatical analysis is the desire to account for more sophisticated aspects of linguistic usage. However, the position is very different when one moves to the stronger definition of competence as representing the internalized knowledge of the native speaker. In this case, contrary evidence about language usage might lead to different conclusions about the form of rules which underly language performance.

Summary

Competence and performance

Competence, in the sense of what it means to know a language, is defined by the grammar of a language; *performance* refers to the actual utterances made by the language users. A speaker's performance, including his linguistic intuitions, does not always give a true reflection of the linguistic rules of the language. This raises problems both for determining linguistic data and for the attempt to base psychological models of the language user on linguistic analysis.

Weaker and stronger implications of competence/performance distinction

Weaker definition: transformational grammar provides the best description of linguistic output in terms of generative rules that meet the three levels of adequacy criteria (see p. 34). A psychological model of the language user must provide an account of the operations (not necessarily incorporating the rules of the grammar) by which a speaker produces and understands this output.

Stronger definition: transformational grammar describes the rules which are internalized in the speaker and provide the basis for his ability to produce and understand language. A psychological model of the language user must put to the test the hypothesis that speakers are making use of transformational rules when producing and understanding language.

5 Research Based on 1957 Version of Chomsky's Theory

Introduction

The experiments arising out of the 1957 version of transformational theory were based on the strong hypothesis that the generative rules of the grammar are the actual rules used by speakers to produce and understand sentences. The next section will describe the rationale behind the original experiments designed by George Miller to test the psychological reality of transformational rules. However, as further experiments were carried out, it became obvious that the results could not be accounted for solely in terms of syntactic transformational operations. Rather than falling back on a vague appeal to performance variables, two main theoretical approaches were developed to try and account for the failure to find an exact one-to-one correspondence between predictions based on transformational complexity and subjects' performance.

These two approaches offer an interesting contrast in their treatment of the same experimental findings. The research described on page 116 ff is concerned with the extent to which performance in psycholinguistic experiments diverges from natural language usage. Since in 'real life' contexts the only purpose of syntactic rules is to convey semantic relationships, the proposal is that discrepancies in performance with transformations can be explained in terms of whether the transformations are being used to perform their natural semantic function. In contrast to this, the purpose of the models detailed on page 121ff is to investigate the decision-making strategies used by subjects when they attempt to meet the requirements of experimental tasks, even though these may often be different from those involved in ordinary language use. In the final section I argue that a comparison of these approaches necessitates a reconsideration of the operations involved in language processing. It highlights in particular the crucial importance of the interaction between syntactic and semantic processes in a psychological model of language.

Experiments with transformations

The chief attraction of Chomsky's 1957 theory for psychologists was the possibility that generative rules are the same as those used by speakers to produce sentences. However, when it came to looking at the phrase structure rules of the grammar, as represented by the rewriting rules given on page 35, it seemed most implausible that people produce sentences by starting with an abstract axiom S, then proceeding to rewrite it as VP and NP and so on, inserting the actual words only at the end of the process. Such a series of operations runs counter to every intuition that people start with 'what they want to say' and only then generate an appropriate sentence to express it. Incidentally, the introduction into the 1965 version of the lexicon and lexical rules for inserting words into phrase structure strings still leaves this fundamental difficulty unresolved, a problem to which we shall return in the next chapter.

A more hopeful line of attack was to concentrate on the transformational component of the grammar; and the first experiments carried out by George Miller and his associates were designed to test the psychological reality of kernel sentences and transformations. As explained in Chapter 2, transformational rules, strictly speaking, operate on terminal strings output by the phrase structure component rather than on actual kernel sentences, since even these require a minimum number of obligatory transformations. For purposes of exposition, however, there has been a tendency to treat kernel sentences as being directly generated by phrase structure rewriting rules (see Figure 1), while more complex sentences are produced by performing transformations on these kernel sentences.

This was the basis for George Miller's proposal that when speakers produce complex sentences they do so by first generating a kernel sentence and then applying a number of optional transformations. Conversely, a listener who hears a complex sentence has to undo these optional transformations in order to retrieve the kernel. This implies that he cannot understand the sentence without carrying out this detransformational analysis. The main experimental hypothesis that follows from this is that each type of transformation is an individual operation that takes a certain measurable amount of time to carry out. A further prediction is that, when several transformations are needed to produce a complex sentence, the times taken for the individual transformations will be additive; thus showing that the operations are independent and carried out one after the other.

In order to test these hypotheses Miller and McKean (1964) used a sentence matching task in which each transformational relationship could be investigated individually. For instance, for the active to passive transformation, subjects were presented with a series of sentences, half of which were in the active form and half in the passive. They were told beforehand that they would be required to turn an active into its equivalent passive or vice versa, and then to find the corresponding transformed sentence in a search list of sentences. They were given each sentence separately and asked to press a button when they had made the necessary transformation and were ready for the search list of sentences. Although both transformation and search times were recorded, the focus of the experiment was on the times taken by subjects to carry out the various transformations. A control condition was included, in which subjects had to search for sentences identical to those presented, thus controlling the time taken just to read the sentences. By subtracting these reading times it was hoped that the remaining time would be a pure measure of transformation time.

Two transformations were tested, the passive and the negative, giving six transformational relationships as follows:

Passive	active affirmative	↔	passive affirmative
Transformation	(AA)		(PA)
	active negative	↔	passive negative
	(AN)		(PN)

Negative	active affirmative	↔	active negative
Transformation	(AA)		(AN)
	passive affirmative	↔	passive negative
	(PA)		(PN)
Passive and	active affirmative	↔	passive negative
Negative	(AA)		(PN)
Transformations	active negative	↔	passive affirmative
	(AN)		(PA)

An example of AA–PN might be the sentence *Jane liked the small boy* which would have to be transformed into *The small boy was not liked by Jane*.

As Miller points out, it is only through transformational analysis that the pairs of sentence types would be presented in this way, with the AA–PA and AN–PN relations, for instance, being grouped together as both being examples of the passive transformation.

The results shown in Table 1 provide impressive evidence in support of Miller's predictions. The times taken for the two examples of the negative and passive transformations were reasonably consistent, although with a slight tendency for the transformations involving AA sentences to be slightly quicker in each case. Moreover, while the figures in Table 1 are for

Table 1 **Data from Miller and McKean** (1964)
Transformation times (corrected for reading times)

Transformation	Sentence types	Seconds	
	AA – PA	0.81	
Passive			0.91
	AN – PN	1.01	
	AA – AN	0.40	
Negative			0.41
	PA – PN	0.42	
Passive and	AA – PN	1.24	
Negative			1.53
	AN – PA	1.82	

combined transformations and detransformations for each pair of sentence types, Miller and McKean report that the time taken to carry out an operation was much the same regardless of whether it was a transformation or a detransformation (i.e. AA to PA took the same time as PA to AA). This supports the notion that encoding and decoding are mirror image processes. Concerning the prediction about additivity of times, if one adds together the times taken for the passive and negative transformations, the sum is not far off the time for the double passive and negative transformation. This is evidence in favour of the proposal that transformations are individual operations that are carried out independently and serially during the encoding or decoding of a sentence. Finally, it should be noted that, of the single transformations, the passive transformation took longer than the negative.

I have described this experimental approach in some detail because it represents the clearest example of deriving a performance model directly from syntactic operations, a clarity that diminished rapidly in succeeding experiments as the effect of an increasing number of non-syntactic factors became apparent. However, a major criticism of this experiment, in spite of the impressive orderliness of its findings, is that subjects were actually asked to make the transformations and detransformations. While the results show that people can perform such operations when required to do so, and that measures of the times taken to do so reveal interesting and consistent differences, there is no proof that this is what people do when normally producing sentences.

To try to tap transformational operations more indirectly, subjects were asked to memorize sentences of different transformational complexity. The supposition was that they would detransform the sentences and store the kernel, plus a 'footnote' about the transformations required to reconstitute the sentence into its original form. An ingenious technique for measuring the amount of memory storage space required for various types of sentences was devised by Savin and Perchonock (1965). They asked their subjects to recall an aurally presented sentence and a number of unrelated words presented after the sentence. If the sentence was correctly recalled the number of single words that could also be remembered was taken as an index of the amount of extra memory space still available after the sentence had been decoded. They presented their subjects with a variety of sentence types, including passives, negatives and questions, and combinations of these transformations. It was found that the number of extra words recalled was a direct function of the presence of additional transformations, with fewer words being remembered after the more complex sentences. Further, the increment in storage space used up for each transformation was fairly consistent, independently of the other transformations present (i.e. the differences between AA and PA, AN and PN and Q and PQ, all representing the passive transformation, were roughly equal).

These results were in line with those of the Miller and McKean experiment in that performance is again directly related to the number of transformations to be processed. There are certain difficulties, however, about this straightforward interpretation. For one thing, in this experiment the extra storage space needed for the negative transformation was larger than that for the passive transformation. As Savin and Perchonock point out, there is no basis for predicting the relative difficulty of individual transformations of different types; but it seems odd that, whereas in the Miller and McKean experiment the negative transformation took less time than the passive, here it took up more storage space. In spite of the different measures being used, one might at least expect the same rank order of increasing complexity due to particular transformations.

Another difficulty with the sentence recall paradigm is lack of certainty about what is actually stored by subjects. Since they were asked for *verbatim* recall, subjects could have been trying to remember the sentences as they stood, without any decoding into kernels and transformational 'footnotes' or tags. One argument against this is that one would then expect length of sentence to be a crucial variable. Savin and Perchonock report that, while complex sentences with more transformations tend to be longer than simple sentences, the pattern of results cannot be explained solely in this way. For instance, the questions were no longer than the kernels, and sometimes even shorter, and yet took up more storage space.

Further evidence in favour of transformational tags comes from an experiment by Mehler (1963). He looked at errors in recalling sentences to see whether these could be explained in terms of tags being forgotten, which would lead to sentences being remembered in a simpler less-transformed form. He found a tendency for complex sentences to be remembered in kernel form more often than the other way round. Moreover, while not all sentence errors were in the direction of a less-transformed form, a plausible explanation was that the subjects, who knew that there were several sentence types in each set, made a guess as to whether a tag had been there or not, thus sometimes adding rather than dropping a transformation. There was also some indication that there was more likelihood of just one transformation being added or deleted incorrectly rather than two or three at once.

However, there still remains the problem that in *verbatim* recall experiments the meaning of the sentences is not strictly relevant to the subject's task. Consequently, they are not a real test of the hypothesis that subjects have to decode sentences into kernels in order to be able to *understand* them. This was the motivation behind a series of experiments in which subjects had to decide whether sentences were true or false, the assumption being that in order to evaluate the truth value of sentences they would have to understand their meaning. The prediction, then, was that evaluation times would be a function of the number of transformations required to decode sentences into kernel form.

The general experimental design (McMahon, 1963, Slobin, 1966, Gough, 1965, 1966) was for subjects to be presented with statements such as *The girl is hitting the boy*, which they had to judge as true or false in relation to a pictured situation which might or might not show a girl hitting a boy. The statements were in the form of active affirmative (AA), negative (AN), passive (PA) and passive negative sentences (PN).

The overall findings show that kernels are the easiest to deal with, sentences with single transformations next, while passive negative sentences take longest to evaluate. These findings again support the idea that response times are a function of the number of transformational operations. However, certain aspects of the data fit in less well with the idea that each individual transformation takes a consistent amount of time to carry out and that this is done serially and independently of other operations. First, it was found that negative sentences took longer to evaluate than passive sentences, although it had been the passive transformation that took longer in Miller and McKean's transformation matching task. A further complication was that, even allowing for this crossover, the times for negatives and passives did not have a constant value but varied in relation to whether the sentences were true or false. Thus, whereas true AA and PA sentences tended to be considerably easier than false AAs and PAs, with AN and PN sentences the trend was in the opposite direction with false negatives taking the same or less time than true negatives. Clearly, this goes right against the hypothesis that each transformation takes a constant amount of time to perform. More seriously, it contradicts the idea that sentences have to be detransformed in order to be understood. This follows since, if all detransformations have to be carried out prior to any consideration of meaning, there should be no interaction between type of transformation and the semantic factor of truth and falsehood.

So the real difficulty for the transformational hypothesis is that its predictions are fully confirmed only when language is being used artificially, as in Miller's transformation experiment and the *verbatim* recall tasks. When subjects are performing the more natural language function of extracting meaning from sentences, any exact one-to-one correspondence between transformational complexity and performance disappears. Not only does the relative difficulty of the negative and passive transformations alter under different circumstances but this in turn interacts with the semantic factor of truth value.

One obviously relevant factor is that, in addition to purely syntactic considerations of transformational complexity, the optional transformations of the 1957 theory differ in that some alter meaning while others leave meaning unchanged. Extreme examples are the negative, which expresses the opposite of its kernel sentence, and the passive, which preserves the semantic content of the kernel. Question and imperative transformations represent changes in what linguists call the modal significance of the kernel sentence.

As Miller and others have pointed out, in a transformation matching task like Miller and McKean's, semantic factors such as these might not be expected to have much effect on subjects' performance. However, in any experiment in which subjects have to consider the meaning of sentences, meaning changes such as that associated with the negative transformation would have to be taken into account. Thus, in the evaluation experiments it is not surprising that negatives are found to be more difficult than passives; with the former one must keep track of the transformational meaning change, while with passives the meanings of sentence and kernel are the same.

Other indications that semantic factors might be involved appear in an evaluation experiment by Slobin (1966) which used both reversible and non-reversible actives and passives. The reversible sentences were those in which either noun could just as well be subject or object, e.g. *The boy was hit by the girl*; the non-reversible those in which it would be anomalous to change round subject and object, e.g. *The girl is watering the flowers*. Another way of putting this is that *The girl is being watered by the flowers* breaks certain selection restrictions on the kind of subject and object that can occur with the verb *waters*. Slobin found that these non-reversible passives took no longer to evaluate than equivalent actives, and argues that this is because, regardless of the form of the sentence, it is obvious which of the two nouns is subject and which object. It is difficult to explain this equivalence of active and passive evaluation times in terms of the transformational hypothesis, which implies that detransformation of passives into kernels should be a necessary first step before semantic cues can be taken into account.

In the light of this evidence, Miller concludes that virtually all the time taken to process sentences is concerned with semantic operations. Consequently, in evaluation experiments only the meaning change entailed by the negative would be expected to cause trouble, while the passive would need no extra semantic processing, except possibly when there are no obvious semantic cues as to which noun is subject and which object. Miller even goes so far as to say that the longer times taken to transform passives in the Miller and McKean experiment must have been due to some artifact concerned with the peculiar requirements of the experimental task. The pessimistic conclusion that might be drawn from all this is that, in so far as psycholinguistic experiments are able to demonstrate effects due to transformational complexity, they are by definition artificial since in normal language it is semantic factors that predominate. Realization of this psycholinguistic dilemma has stimulated the attempts to solve it which will form the topic of the following sections.

Experiments on semantic function

The reasoning behind this line of research is that neither syntax nor semantics can be considered in isolation, since the only purpose of using different syntactic transformations is to communicate some particular aspect of meaning. When tranformations are being used to perform this natural function of conveying a meaning relationship (as they normally are in natural language) they will be produced and understood perfectly easily. The special difficulties with them in psycholinguistic experiments are explained by the fact that transformations are being used in contexts in which they are not performing their natural semantic function. The main concern of this approach, then, is to try and isolate the semantic contexts which facilitate performance with each type of syntactic transformation. The idea is that this will provide clues to the 'real life' situations in which they are used naturally and easily to perform a particular semantic function.

A pioneer experiment in this field by Wason (1965) investigated the contexts in which it would be natural to use a negative. This transformation was found to cause maximum disruption of performance in the evaluation tasks described in the last section. However, if it were *always* more difficult than the affirmative, one might have expected it to disappear altogether as a result of linguistic natural selection. Its survival seems to indicate that there must be some occasions when it is used to perform a special semantic function. Wason suggested that one 'context of plausible denial', as he termed it, is when a negative is used to correct a misconception. There is more reason to say *The train was not late this morning* if the train normally is late, thus denying the mistaken expectancy that it was late this morning as usual. Similarly, one would not expect someone to take longer to understand the negative *I am not going to work today* than the affirmative *I am going to work today*. Indeed, assuming that the speaker's normal practice is daily work, the negative conveys more information by denying something the speaker might normally expect.

To test this hypothesis, Wason designed an ingenious experiment in which subjects were presented with an array of eight numbered circles, seven of which were red while one (say Circle 4) was blue. Since the blue Circle 4 is an exceptional item, there is more likely to be a misconception that it might be red; and the prediction was that it would be natural to use a negative to correct this mistaken expectancy. This was confirmed by the finding that subjects took less time to complete the sentence *Circle 4 is not . . . . (red)* than the sentence *Circle 7 is not . . . . (blue)*.

An extension of the function of the negative to cover, not only cases in which the negative is used to correct a *mistaken* prior assertion, but *all* denials of a prior assertion whether true or false, was suggested by Greene (1970, a, b). This proposal that the function of the negative is to reverse meaning states more than the obvious logical relation. What is being claimed is that the negative is concerned with a relationship *between* two propositions, the negative statement and a prior assertion. An affirmative, on the other hand, carries no special implications about prior assertions. In other words, choice of the negative form indicates that the speaker is not merely stating a proposition but doing so in relation to some presupposition, whether an overt prior assertion or an unstated expectancy. As Clark has put it in a recent paper (1970), 'a speaker makes an assumption about the beliefs (or apparent beliefs) of his listener whenever he utters a denial'.

The point being argued is illustrated by 'real life' occasions when the important thing is to emphasize that some presumptive assertion is *not* the case. Examples of such negatives would be *I did not intend to be unkind* or *Not guilty*, whether they happen to be objectively true or false. It is interesting, too, that in English there is no special construction for making an affirmative contradiction of a *negative* prior assertion; one has to use emphasis and/or the auxiliary *do*, as in '*But I* did *shut the door*' in reply to *You didn't shut the door*. In some languages however, there is a special form of the affirmative for performing the function of denying a prior negative assertion. In French, for instance, the use of *oui*, the normal word for *yes*, would imply agreement as in *Yes, I didn't shut the door*, whereas the use of *si* would imply the denial *Yes, I did shut the door*. This difference in usage indicates that there is a real difference between assertion and denial.

It follows from this argument that, if the function of the negative is to signal a denial or contradiction, then negatives should be facilitated in a context in which they are used to change meaning. In order to test this prediction, Greene carried out an experiment in which subjects had to decide whether pairs of sentences had the same or a different meaning. She found that (given that x and y are different numbers) subjects took less time to decide that the following sentences have a *different* meaning:

x exceeds y
x does not exceed y

than that the following two sentences have the *same* meaning:

y exceeds x
x does not exceed y.

This result was interpreted as providing support for the view that performance with the negative is facilitated when it is being used to perform its natural function of signalling a change of meaning.

Pairs of active and passive sentences were included as a control and in this case there was no facilitation of sentence pairs with different meanings. Indeed, if anything, the different meaning pair:

x exceeds y
x is exceeded by y

tended to be more difficult than the same meaning pair:

y exceeds x
x is exceeded by y.

A further point is that the first 'different meaning' negative pair took less time to evaluate than either of the active and passive pairs, showing that when it is being used in a meaning change role the negative causes no special difficulty. This is in contrast to the results of other evaluation experiments in which negatives were always found to be more difficult than passives.

Turning to the function of the passive transformation, the assumption of the Greene experiment was that it is not concerned with meaning change. Like other stylistic variations which apparently do not change the semantic content of a proposition, the problem is to specify what role it plays in the language. Some recent research has shown, however, that without necessarily changing the meaning of a statement as a whole, use of the passive form may carry implications about the relative importance of the logical subject and object. Johnson-Laird (1968) investigated this using a task in which subjects had to choose between different syntactic forms of a statement in order to communicate a difference in the relative sizes of coloured areas. When they were trying to convey that there was a difference in size between the logical subject and object, subjects tended to choose a passive rather than an active form of the descriptive statement. Normally the use of the passive brings the logical object towards the front of the

sentence; and it was this form that was preferred when subjects wanted to emphasize the colour described by the logical
object, as in *There is a* red *area that is preceded by a blue area*.
Interestingly, when they wanted to emphasize the logical subject they still chose a passive but this time the odd inverted
form *There is a* blue *area that a red area is preceded by* rather
than the straightforward active *There is a blue area that pre-
cedes a red area.* Johnson-Laird argues that the function of the
passive is both to draw attention to differential emphasis being
placed on the logical subject and object and to indicate this
emphasis by changing the word order.

Other experiments have also found that use of the passive
increases the relative importance of the logical object. Clark
(1965) showed that, when people were asked to fill in blanks in
active and passive sentence-frames, more animate nouns were
used to fill in the logical object position in passive than in
active sentences. A similar result was found in an experiment
by Johnson (1967) in which ratings of activity and potency on
the semantic differential (Osgood et al., 1957) were taken for
nonsense syllables in the subject and object positions in active
and passive sentences. The fact that ratings for the subject and
object positions were much closer together in the passive than
in the active sentences again indicates a difference in the significance of the logical object in a passive sentence.

From all this evidence it seems plausible that use of a passive like *The dog is being chased by the cat* in place of the kernel form *The cat chases the dog* represents a shift in interest
from the logical subject *cat* to the logical object *dog*. Undoubtedly, choice of a particular form for expressing a statement is determined by a great number of factors, including,
for instance, stylistic conventions about the use of passives
in academic prose! Nevertheless, the research strategy of
looking at performance in relation to the use of alternative
snytactic forms in different semantic contexts has thrown
some light on factors that might affect their occurrence in
natural language.

The next question to be considered is what sort of explanation this approach might offer for the findings of the evalua-

tion experiments reported in the last section, in particular the unexpected interaction between negation and truth value. As indicated earlier, in many of those experiments it was found that, while true affirmatives were easier to deal with than false affirmatives, with negative sentences it was the true sentences that were more difficult than the false sentences.

From the point of view of the semantic function hypothesis, it could be argued that it is the *false* negatives that are performing the function of signalling a change of meaning, in the sense that they are *denying* the situation shown in the picture. The *true* negatives, on the other hand, are being used to perform the unnatural non-meaning change role of affirming what *is* in the picture. This would account for the fact that true negatives were found to be more difficult than false negatives. In the case of affirmatives, of course, one would expect the opposite finding that true assertions are easier to deal with than false affirmatives used to deny a state of affairs. Plausible as this suggestion may seem, however, it should be pointed out that an alternative explanation for the interaction between negation and truth value has been proposed in terms of an information processing model, to which we will turn in the next section.

Information processing models

The information processing approach relies on essentially the same basic facts about negatives as were discussed in the last section. But instead of concentrating on their usage in natural language, the aim is to account for the findings of the evaluation experiments by looking at the actual operations a subject might carry out to arrive at the required truth value decisions. Two models that are similar in several respects have been proposed by Trabasso (1970, in press) and Clark (1970, in press, Chase and Clark, 1972, Clark and Chase, in press). Both models assume that people start off with a tendency to respond 'true' and alter this response if necessary as processing continues. Both models make the further assumption that at some point the subject compares the sentence against a coding of the pictured situation, which takes the form of an affirmative representation such as *The cat is chasing the dog*. The main question at issue is how the subject codes the sentence in order to carry out comparison with this picture coding.

According to what Clark calls the 'conversion' model of negation, and what I shall term Trabasso's 'translation' model, it is proposed that the subject translates negative sentences into an equivalent affirmative coding (see Steps 1 and 2 in Figure 9). For instance, the negative *The dog is not chasing the cat* would be translated into *The cat is chasing the dog*. Having carried out this conversion the subject compares this coding against his affirmative coding of the picture, say, *The cat is chasing the dog* (Steps 3 and 4). If the subject, object and verb features of the two codings match, as in this case, the response is kept as 'true'; if the features do not match the response will be changed to 'false' (Step 5).

This version of the model predicts that negatives will take longer than affirmatives because of the initial translation of negatives into equivalent affirmatives. However, once this has been done TAs and translated TNs should be faster than FAs and translated FNs. This is because it is the *true* statements that will match the picture coding, therefore needing no adjustment of response, while it is the *false* statements that will involve a mismatch and a consequent change of response. Looking at the operations given for all four types of sentence in Figure 9, TAs would be expected to be the quickest because they involve neither translation nor a mismatch of features leading to a change of response. FNs would be the most difficult because they involve both these operations. FAs need no translation but do involve a mismatch while TNs need translation but do not produce a mismatch. In order to arrive at an overall rank order of difficulty of TA, FA, TN, FN, the additional assumption is necessary that the operation of translating negatives, as required for TNs, takes longer than the operation of changing response as a result of mismatch, as required for FAs.

As both Trabasso and Clark point out, such translation or conversion of negatives is only feasible when the situation is a binary one. This follows from the fact that in normal circum-

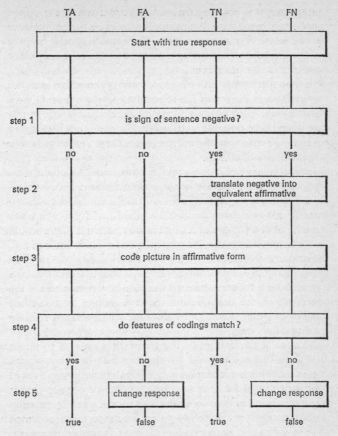

Figure 9 'Conversion' or 'translation' model of negation

stances a negative only specifies what is *not* the case but gives no indication of what *is* the case. Consequently, there is no basis for converting it into any one particular affirmative. In a situation in which there are only two possibilities, however, negatives and affirmatives become equivalent in this respect. In a binary situation to affirm one possibility is the same as denying the other possibility. Similarly, a negative statement that one event is not the case amounts to an assertion that the other event is the case. An example would be the equivalence of *The number is not even* and *The number is odd*, both of which affirm that the number is odd rather than the only other possibility of its being even.

In the experiments with pictures, some of the verbal material was artificially binary in the sense that only two events were possible, say, a dog chasing a cat or a cat chasing a dog. In this case it would be possible to translate *The dog is not chasing the cat* into *The cat is chasing the dog*, since these are the only two possible states of affairs.

In non-binary conditions, on the other hand, following such a procedure might give you the wrong answer. If one translated *The dog is not chasing the cat* into the equivalent affirmative *The cat is chasing the dog* and then had to compare the latter against a picture of a dog chasing a mouse, there would be a mismatch between the sentence and picture codings and the response would be changed to false. However, the original negative *The dog is not chasing the cat* is in actual fact *true* of a dog chasing a mouse, since all that the negative denies is the one event of the dog chasing the cat, leaving an unlimited number of other possibilities amongst which the cat chasing the dog is only one.

Because of this failure of the translation method to retain all the information given by the original negative, Clark argues that this is a cheating way of dealing with negatives in contrast to what he calls the 'true' model of negation. This is essentially equivalent to Trabasso's model when translation is not possible (see Figure 10). As before the picture is assumed to be given an affirmative coding (Step 3). However, negatives, instead of being translated into affirmatives, are coded in a negative form such as (*false* (*dog chases cat*)) (Steps 1 and 2). The next step is to compare this sentence coding against the picture coding (Step 4). If the features in the inner bracket match with those of the picture coding, the 'true' response is left unaltered but if there is a mismatch it is changed to 'false' (Step 5). At the next stage the signs of the two codings are compared and, since the picture coding is by definition affirmative, comparison

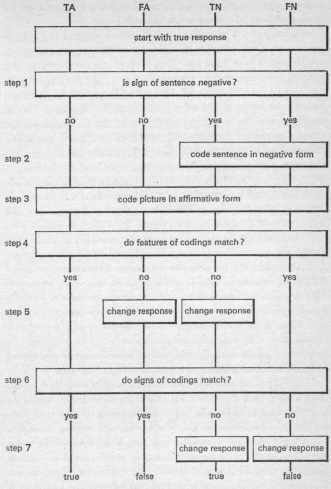

Figure 10 'True' model of negation

with a negative (false) sentence will involve a mismatch and a further change of response (Steps 6 and 7).

According to this model it is FNs which require less operations than TNs. To take an example, when the FN *The dog is not chasing the cat*, coded as (*false* (*dog chases cat*)), is matched against a picture coding *The dog is chasing the cat* the subject, object and verb features of the two codings will be found to match and no response adjustment will be necessary. At the second stage the negative (false) sign of the sentence will involve a mismatch with the affirmative picture coding and the response will be changed to 'false'. This means that only one response changing operation has been required. In the case of the TN *The cat is not chasing the dog*, coded as (*false* (*cat chases dog*)), there will be a mismatch of features when it is compared with the picture coding *The dog is chasing the cat* and the response will be altered from 'true' to 'false'. When a mismatch between the negative and affirmative signs is discovered at the next stage the response will be readjusted back to 'true'. TNs consequently involve two response alterations as compared to one for FNs. It should be noted, too, that this model will cover the non-binary case since, if the TN *The dog is not chasing the cat* is compared with a picture coding *The dog is chasing a mouse*, a mismatch in features will still occur resulting in a change of response to 'false'; this will then be readjusted when the negative and affirmative signs are found to be different, to give a correct final response of 'true'.

When considering the overall rank order of difficulty, again TAs would be expected to be easiest because there would be no mismatch at either the features matching or sign comparison stages. But this time TNs would take the longest since two response changing operations are required. FAs would need one change of response as a result of a mismatch of coding features, while FNs would require one change of response as a result of a mismatch of negative and affirmative signs. In a series of experiments Clark and his associates have shown that 'negation time', including initial coding and mismatch of signs, takes longer than what he calls 'falsification time', by which he means the times taken to evaluate a mismatch of features as in the case of the FAs and TNs. This differential effect due to negation would account for the fact that FNs take longer than FAs although both involve only one change of response.

To sum up, both Trabassos's and Clark's models propose two possible sets of operations for evaluating the truth value of verbal statements, one (Clark's 'conversion' model), which predicts an order of increasing difficulty of TA, FA, TN, FN, and the other (Clark's 'true' model), which predicts a rank order of TA, FA, FN, TN. It is the latter model which accounts for the interaction between negation and truth value, since it predicts that FNs will be easier than TNs. The main question, then, is under what circumstances people use one or other of these strategies.

It is clear from his use of the terms 'true' and 'conversion' that Clark considers the model in which negatives are coded in a negative form for comparison with the picture coding a more accurate reflection of what goes on in the normal processing of negatives. Trabasso's account, on the other hand, in concentrating on optional strategies that might be open to subjects, tends to assume that the conversion or translation method will be used unless it is for some reason not feasible. Trabasso suggests two circumstances when this might be the case: first, when the verbal material is not binary, and, secondly, when the sentence is presented simultaneously with or after the picture instead of before it. As pointed out earlier, translation of negatives is only possible in a binary situation. In addition, it is suggested that when sentences are presented with or after the picture, the subject would be likely to go ahead with comparing a sentence in its negative form without bothering to translate it into an affirmative, even were this possible.

In support of the first of these arguments, Trabasso cites some experiments by Gough (1965, 1966) in which the sentence material could not be treated as binary, since a sentence such as *The boy is not hitting the girl* might have to be verified against a picture showing not the binary opposite of a girl hitting a boy but other possible events such as a boy *kicking* a girl. Under these circumstances, in which translation of negatives into equivalent binary affirmatives is impossible, FNs were found to be quicker than TNs as predicted by the non-translation 'true' model. On the second point, some ex-periments by Trabasso, Rollins and Shaughnessy (1971) demonstrate the effect of varying the order in which the verbal description and picture are presented. When the description came *before* the picture TNs were quicker than FNs in line with the translation model, but when the description came *after* the picture FNs were quicker than TNs as predicted by the 'true' model involving direct comparison of negatives.

However, looking at the results of the evaluation experi-ments as a whole, it is clear that more important than order of presentation was the factor of how subjects regarded the requirements of the experiment. Variables such as the amount of time given for processing the sentences, opportunities for practice, instructions and the type of material used all had an effect on the strategies subjects developed for dealing with the task. In general, the further removed the task and material from natural language use, the more likely subjects were to follow the conversion strategy of translating negatives into equivalent affirmatives rather than dealing with them directly in their negative form. For example, in the Trabasso, Rollins and Shaughnessy experiments, which produced results in accordance with the conversion model, subjects were given as long as they liked to process the verbal description before pressing a button to present the picture. Further, subjects were extremely well practised (in one case a subject dealt with over 8000 descriptions during a period of 40 days), thus giving them plenty of opportunity to develop the strategy of trans-lating negatives. This was all the more likely since the descrip-tions were not sentences but lexical items such as *orange and not small*, *not green and large*, which had to be evaluated against coloured patches. It must soon have become obvious that only two colours and sizes were being used, making it safe to translate *not green* into *orange*, and so on.

Compare this with an experiment carried out by Slobin (1966) which ought to have obtained the same results, since the sentences were presented before the pictures, and were binary in the sense that each sentence was confirmed or falsified by only two possible events. However, a procedural difference was that the experimenter exposed the picture after saying the sentence, thus not allowing unlimited time for processing the sentence. Moreover, as subjects were faced with the more 'natural' situation of being presented with twenty-four different pictures, it might not have appeared so obvious that each negative could be translated into its equivalent binary affirmative, particularly as passive and passive negative sentences were also being tested. In the event the adult subjects in Slobin's experiment produced data in accordance with the translation model, while the children performed according to the 'true' model.

In Greene's experiment (described on p. 118) it was also the case that, since the sentence pairs were binary and presented simultaneously, subjects could have carried out a translation of negatives into affirmatives. However, not only were the overall results in line with the non-translation 'true' model, but subjects reported a clear distinction between 'immediate' appreciation of the meaning relationships between 'natural' pairs, as compared with other more difficult pairs which they had to 'work out' by a series of translation and decision making operations.

Rather similar results were obtained in some experiments by Wason (1961) which required subjects to evaluate statements with a known truth value, such as *7 is not an even number*. As the subject is already in possession of the objective facts about oddness and evenness of numbers, one might assume that this is equivalent to the case in which the pictured situation is presented before the sentence. However, the important variable appears to have been whether the task was a verification one, as in the case of all the other experiments discussed here, or whether it was a construction task in which subjects had to complete sentences like . . . . *is not an even number* in order to make them true or false. While in the verification task TNs and FNs took about the same amount of time, and FNs less time in another similar experiment by Wason and Jones (1963), in the construction task FNs were more difficult than TNs. Here, as Wason points out, the instruction to fill in a number to make a negative false involves a double operation, unless subjects realize that negation and falsity cancel out (in the above example filling in an *even* number like 8 allows for both negation and falsity). In the verification task, on the other hand, some subjects reported a strategy of converting, say, *7 is not even* into *7 is odd*, while other subjects reported that they used a method of direct comparison of the negative statement against their knowledge of whether the number was really even or odd, thus approximating to the 'true' model.

A final example of how much the effect depends on the strategy adopted by the subject is provided by some experiments by Young and Chase (1971). In one condition subjects were asked to translate negatives into equivalent affirmatives. Under these instructions subjects' responses conformed to the conversion model with TNs being faster than FNs. But with no conversion instructions in an otherwise identical experiment, the 'true' model prediction of FNs being faster than TNs was found.

The conclusion seems to be that subjects will try to develop problem solving strategies appropriate to the experimental task, some of which may be quite remote from linguistic skills as normally used. It is to the credit of the information processing models that they have drawn attention to the variety of operations subjects may be using. Nevertheless, there still remains in question the extent to which subjects' performance in psycholinguistic experiments reflects natural language processing (for a recent discussion of this point see Wason, 1972). In the next section the original transformational hypothesis will be evaluated in the light of the information processing and semantic function approaches to this problem.

Evaluation of transformational hypothesis

Expressed in its strictest form, the transformational hypothesis predicts an exact one-to-one correspondence between the number of transformational steps involved in the generation of a sentence and the time taken to produce or decode that sentence.

From this it should be possible to arrive at a rank order of difficulty for sentence types based on the number of transformations required to generate them. Since this rank order should be invariant regardless of the circumstances in which sentences are used, the results of the evaluation experiments show that other factors must be involved. Not only were negatives relatively more difficult to deal with than passives as the experimental tasks got more meaningful; but the negative transformation itself took more or less time according to whether sentences were true or false.

The information processing models proposed by Clark and Trabasso set out a series of operations which it is claimed will account for these findings. While both models agree on the type of decision making operations required for comparing sentence and picture codings, the crucial question is how the sentences are coded in the first place. In the conversion model (see Figure 9) it is assumed that negatives are coded into equivalent affirmatives; but, as pointed out earlier, this is only feasible in the special case of a strictly binary situation. Certainly, from the semantic function point of view, this would be just the situation in which it would be pointless to use a negative, since if negatives could always be translated into equivalent affirmatives there would be no justification for their existence. Carrying out such a conversion is to ignore all the special semantic implications of negation.

Looking, then, to the 'true' model (see Figure 10) as a more likely approximation to the normal processing of negatives, one question that can be asked is how the suggested coding of negatives in a form such as (*false* (*dog chases cat*)) relates to the transformational hypothesis of decoding negatives into kernels. Clearly there is a close connection between this type of coding and the kernel plus transformation tag that might be supposed to underly a negative such as (*negative* (*dog chases cat*)). This analysis is reinforced by a consideration of possible codings of passive sentences in an evaluation task. In this case, any direct matching of sentence features against a picture coding would lead to the following odd results.

Applying the 'true' model given in Figure 10, but substituting

TPs and FPs for TNs and FNs, the stages would be: to compare the subject, object and verb features of the sentence coding against the picture coding (adjusting the response to false if there is a mismatch) and then to make a further adjustment of the response if the codings of sentence and picture are differentially signed for being in the passive. There are two difficulties about this procedure. In the first place, it is the true passives (TPs) that would involve a mismatch of features at Step 4 since, for instance, the TP *The cat is being chased by the dog* would have a different order of nouns from the appropriate picture coding *The dog is chasing the cat*. The response would therefore have to be changed to 'false' and later readjusted to 'true' when the sentence was found to be signed for the passive at Step 6, thus involving two response changing operations. On the other hand, it is the FP *The dog is being chased by the cat* which would match the features of the picture coding *The dog is chasing the cat*, and so only one change of response would be necessary as a result of the sentence being signed for the passive. The prediction would follow that TPs are more difficult than FPs, while all the experimental results show the reverse to be the case.

A second difficulty is that in a non-binary situation such direct matching of the untranslated passive might result in the wrong response. To take an example, if the sentence *The dog is being chased by the cat* were to be evaluated against a picture coding *The dog is chasing a mouse*, the response would first be changed to 'false' because of the mismatch of features, and then changed back to 'true' due to the sentence being signed for the passive; whereas the sentence is clearly false.

The interesting thing is that in direct contrast to the negative, for passives it is the non-translation 'true' model that gives the wrong answer, and the conversion model involving translation of passives into equivalent affirmatives that preserves correct truth value relations. Thus, replacing TNs and FNs by TPs and FPs in the conversion model given in Figure 9, the passive *The cat is being chased by the dog* would be translated into the equivalent affirmative *The dog is chasing the cat* (Step 2). This, if true, would match the features of the picture coding *The dog is chasing the cat* and, if false, would be found not to match. Since in this case it would be the FP which would involve the double operation of translation into affirmative and mismatch of features, one would get the correct prediction that FPs take longer than TPs. From this it would seem to follow that the operations carried out by subjects when dealing with passives must involve translation into affirmatives.

The difficulty for the information processing model is to explain why the conversion model should be appropriate for passives and the 'true' model for negatives. However, returning to the transformational hypothesis, the kernel of a passive such as *The cat is being chased by the dog* might be supposed to take the form of a translated equivalent active affirmative plus a passive transformation tag, i.e. (*passive* (*dog chases cat*)). Taking this together with the decoding of negatives into kernels such as (*negative* (*dog chases cat*)) one would arrive at an explanation for the differential results. According to this analysis, negatives would be expected to behave in accordance with the 'true' model, with FNs being easier than TNs. Passives, on the other hand, would be translated and so behave in accordance with the conversion model, FPs being harder than TPs.

Following from this, a reasonable conclusion would be that a combination of the transformational and information processing models provides the best fit for the results of the evaluation experiments. Decoding into kernels is not sufficient on its own, because it leaves out of account the processes involved in making a decision about the truth value of the decoded sentences in relation to the pictures. Consequently, it fails to explain the differential effects involved in evaluating true and false negatives and true and false passives. On the other hand, it is clear from the analysis of how the information processing model would deal with negatives and passives that the initial sentence decoding must take some such form as would be envisaged by the transformational hypothesis, i.e. rendering *The dog is not chasing the cat* and *The cat is being chased by the dog* as (*negative* (*dog chases cat*)) and (*passive* (*dog chases cat*)) respectively. It is only by using codings of this sort that the feature and sign matching stages of the information processing model produce results in line with experimental findings about the relative difficulty of true and false negatives and passives.

One point that should be noted is that, despite the use of Chomsky's 1957 terminology of kernels and transformations, the formulation just given fits in particularly well with the 1965 version of Chomsky's theory. Decoding of sentences into forms such as (*negative* (*dog chases cat*)) and (*passive* (*dog chases cat*)) is exactly equivalent to analysis into deep structures, envisaged in the 1965 theory as containing all the information necessary for semantic interpretation, including transformation markers such as negative and passive. Indeed, as indicated in the above analysis, any other representation would fail to fit the data; especially in the case of the passives when attention to the 'untransformed' surface order of subject and object would result in incorrect matching of features. Moreover, since the evaluation tasks under discussion require not a full semantic interpretation but only a judgement as to whether sentences have the same or a different meaning from the pictured situation, the operations proposed in the information processing model are just those which the semantic component might carry out to arrive at such a decision. According to this line of thought, the extra time for evaluating negatives as compared with passives can be accounted for in the following way. Once decoding into deep structure kernels has been carried out, the semantic component has to take into account the presence of the negative marker because it results in a reversal of meaning; the passive marker, on the other hand, can be ignored because it has no effect on the truth value of a sentence.

This synthesis of the transformational and information processing approaches appears to provide a satisfactory model for subjects' performance in tasks involving evaluation of negatives and passives. Still outstanding, however, is the question of how far this resembles normal language behaviour. For one thing, the combined model relies on the assumption that decoding of sentences has to be completed before any decision making about truth values can begin. In effect, this is the same as Miller's original hypothesis that sentences have to be decoded into their kernels before their meaning can be understood. It is, too, the basis for the 1965 version of transformational grammar in which a complete syntactic analysis of deep structure is required as input to the semantic component.

In opposition to this suggested independence of syntactic and semantic processing is the evidence already quoted from Slobin's experiments using reversible and non-reversible passives. His finding that, when it is semantically obvious which of the nouns is subject and object, as in *The flowers are watered by the girl*, passive sentences take no longer to evaluate than active sentences seems to indicate that people do not always need to carry out a full transformational analysis to arrive at the meaning of a passive. This is confirmed by an experiment by Herriot (1969) using sentences that were non-reversible only in the sense that they described expected events, e.g. *The doctor treated the patient* and *The bather was rescued by the lifeguard*. Although the converse of the sentences was perfectly possible, there was no difference in the times taken by subjects to state the actor and object of active and passive sentences. However, when the subjects and objects were equally likely either way round, as in *The brother hated the sister*, passives took more time than actives. This again supports the view that the passive transformation only takes extra processing time in the absence of clear semantic cues. Moreover, when the non-reversible sentences *were* reversed to give a less likely sentence, subjects tended to get the nouns the wrong way round, e.g., giving the lifeguard as the actor of the sentence *The lifeguard was rescued by the bather*. In other words, they appear to have been paying more attention to semantic cues at the expense of correct syntactic analysis.

Another example of interaction between syntactic and semantic processing is provided by an experiment reported by Schlesinger (1968). He demonstrated that comprehension of nested sentences can be considerably facilitated if semantic cues are available. Subjects found it much easier to grasp the content of a sentence like *This is the hole, that the rat, which our cat, whom the dog bit, made, caught* as compared with a sentence with minimal cues about which noun goes with which verb, as in *This is the boy, that the man, whom the lady, whom our friend saw, knows, hit*. Moreover, as in the Herriot experiment, when the semantic cues are incongruous (as they are if you work it out in the above sentence about the rat, cat and dog), subjects nearly always give an interpretation that is in line with semantic expectations rather than correct syntactic analysis. As Schlesinger points out, embedded sentences of this kind are beyond the capacity of normal linguistic processing without the help of a paper and pencil analysis. Nevertheless, with semantic cues, and perhaps helped by an appropriate context, some meaning may be extracted from them despite the lack of a full syntactic analysis.

To sum up the implications for psychological models of language, the evidence reported in this chapter supports the view that decoding of sentences into kernels or deep structures has a certain psychological reality, in that this appears to be a necessary basis for evaluating the meaning of sentences. What is by no means so clearly demonstrated is that the operations by which people carry out this sentence decoding correspond to the rules given in transformational grammar. For one thing, the 1957 analysis in terms of single transformations for generating negatives and passives is itself an over-simplified version of the many separate transformational steps that might be specified in recent transformational grammars for the generation of complex sentences. For another, the experimental findings indicate that in certain circumstances, such as with the non-reversible passives and embedded sentences, people use non-transformational semantic cues to decode the meanings of sentences. Further evidence is provided by the evaluation experiments, showing that the more the situation approximates to natural language use the more likely subjects are to respond directly to meaning cues, rather than going through an ordered set of transformational and decision making operations. At the same time, it is by no means clear how these cues operate to alert people to the semantic implications of various types of syntactic transformation.

One certain conclusion that can be drawn from all the approaches described in this chapter is the impossibility of considering syntactic analysis independently of the role it plays in analysis of meaning. The advantage of Chomsky's 1965 theory is that, because of the introduction of a semantic component into the grammar itself, problems such as these can be conceptualized within transformational theory.

Summary

Transformation experiments

Experiments to test the strong hypothesis that speakers use transformational rules when matching sentences (Miller and McKean, 1964), memorizing sentences (Savin and Perchonock, 1965, Mehler, 1963) and evaluating the truth value of sentences (McMahon, 1963, Slobin, 1966, Gough, 1965, 1966) failed to find an exact one-to-one correspondence between complexity of transformations and performance, owing to the effect of semantic factors, e.g. variations in performance with negatives and passives according to experimental task and truth value.

Semantic function experiments

Experiments to test the hypothesis that performance with transformed sentences depends on the semantic function for which a transformation is being used (Wason, 1965, Greene, 1970a, b, Johnson-Laird, 1968, Clark, 1965, Johnson, 1967) showed that certain variations in performance could be accounted for in this way, e.g. interaction between negation and truth value.

Information processing models

An information processing model (Trabasso, 1970, Clark, 1970) also accounted for the interaction between negation and truth value, but this was shown to depend on experimental task (Trabasso, Rollins and Shaughnessy, 1971, Wason, 1961, Wason and Jones, 1963, Young and Chase, 1971); and when applied to passives the importance of coding appropriate 'kernels' was demonstrated.

Concluding points

While 'kernel' codings were found to play an important part in sentence processing, doubt was thrown on the hypothesis that a full transformational analysis always needs to be carried out to arrive at the meaning of a sentence (Herriot, 1969, Schlesinger, 1968).

6 Research Based on 1965 Version of Chomsky's Theory

Introduction

As described in the last chapter, the major difficulty that arose with psychological models based on the 1957 concepts of kernels and transformations was the clearly demonstrated effect of semantic factors. While the aim of the 1957 grammar was to account for native speakers' appreciation of relations between sentences, the implication was that this could be explained solely in terms of syntactic analysis. In contrast, the introduction of a set of semantic rules into the 1965 version of the grammar allowed the extraction of semantic content to become a direct concern of linguistic theory. Syntactic analysis is no longer an end in itself but fulfils the function of providing the structural information necessary for arriving at a semantic reading for each sentence.

The tripartite organization of the 1965 theory reflects the traditional concept of language as a code that relates sounds to meaning. The proposal is that sounds are related to meaning through the rules that make up the syntactic component. These generate both a surface structure, which is the input for the phonological component and thus underlies the final sequence of sounds in a sentence, and a deep structure, which is the input for the semantic component and thus underlies the meaning of the sentence. This formalization of the interrelations between syntax, semantics and phonology provides a precise statement of the problem facing any psychological model which attempts to explain the speaker's ability to extract meaning from the sounds he hears and to express his own meaning in sentence form.

The models that will be discussed in the next two sections are based on the assumption that the processes by which the speaker achieves this are centrally concerned with the mapping of surface structures on to deep structures and vice versa. Those described in section 2 make the further assumption that the mapping operations take the same form as the rules of transformational grammar; those in section 3 suggest that other than transformational operations may be utilized. In sections 4 and 5 consideration will be given to models which claim that it would be more parsimonious to suppose that sentence meanings are directly extracted from surface structure, thus by-passing the need for any deep structure analysis at all. In the final two sections a comparison is made between these deep structure and surface structure approaches in the light of their success at providing models of language behaviour.

Transformational deep structure models

The first model to be discussed, that proposed by Katz and Postal in their book *An Integrated Theory of Linguistic Descriptions* (1964), is the one most closely based on the 1965 version of transformational grammar. Not only does it adopt the three components stated in the theory but it attempts also to incorporate the syntactic, phonological and semantic rules that interrelate these components in the exact form in which they appear in the grammar. Like the experiments by Miller described in the last chapter, this is a test of the strong hypothesis that the rules of transformational grammar are operations that are actually performed by language users. Indeed, the Katz and Postal model is an even stricter test of the hypothesis. Whereas the transformational operations postulated in Miller's experiments allowed for the rules being put into reverse, so that sentences could be decoded back into their kernels by undoing the appropriate transformations, Katz and Postal designed their model on the assumption that grammatical rules could operate only in the direction specified by the grammar.

Figure 11 shows a representation adapted from Katz and Postal of the interrelations between the components of the grammar. It will be seen that this is identical to the account given in Chomsky's 1965 theory (see Figure 3 on page 56), except for the box with dotted lines which will be commented on later. Also in Katz and Postal's original diagram there was a dictionary in the semantic component as well as a lexicon in the syntactic component, although in the 1965 theory Chomsky writes of the lexicon as containing semantic as well as syntactic features. This makes no essential difference, however, since it means that in the later version as shown in Figures 3 and 11, the deep structure is input to the semantic component with semantic 'dictionary' features already attached to the words. The semantic component would then operate to combine these semantic features to arrive at the meaning of the whole sentence. Similarly, the surface structure would have phonological features of words already assigned for input to the phonological component.

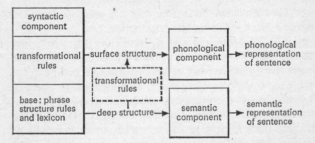

Figure 11

When it comes to devising a psychological model for speech perception and production based on this arrangement the first difficulty is that the syntactic component is the only generative source in the system. The semantic and phonological components are purely interpretative in the sense that they operate on the output of the syntactic rules. Moreover, since the syntactic rules generate strings on an essentially random basis, how is the speaker able to choose a particular string to express his meaning and how does a listener select the string which is appropriate to the sequence of sounds that he hears?

To cope with these problems Katz and Postal propose an analysis-by-synthesis model. By this is meant a system which analyses input strings not directly, but by generating, or synthesizing, strings of equal length until it happens to produce one that matches the input string. Thus, when a sequence of sounds is heard the syntactic component starts generating surface structure strings for input to the phonological component until a phonological representation is produced that matches the incoming sounds. It should be noted that limitation of this generative process to strings of the same length or number of units as the input string begs the question of how sound sequences are segmented into appropriate units.

The next stage in the model would be for the syntactic component to assign a deep structure to the surface structure selected at the first stage. Katz and Postal argue that this is unlikely to be an analysis-by-synthesis process since this would entail generating all the intermediate phrase structure markers between deep and surface structure resulting from the operation of each individual transformation.

A more serious problem with the model as it has been formulated so far is that strictly speaking it is only the phrase structure rules that are truly generative, since according to the 1965 theory transformations are determined by markers in deep structure and therefore can add nothing new to the output of the phrase structure rules. Consequently, even to arrive at the first stage allocation of surface structure it would be necessary to start with the phrase structure rules. These would generate deep structures including the obligatory transformation markers necessary to produce surface structures for matching against the incoming string. In other words, generation of surface structures would have to proceed via deep structure as shown by the dotted section in Figure 11. It would seem to follow from this that, since the deep structure of the final matching surface structure must have been generated in the first place, it would already be available and so there would be no need for Katz and Postal's second stage assignment of deep structure.

In any case, the third stage would be for the deep structure to be fed into the semantic component, to be operated on by Katz and Fodor type rules to arrive at a semantic reading for the sentence. This would be equivalent to the listener understanding the input sentence.

For speech production the process would work the other way round. Presuming that the speaker starts with a semantic representation, or 'idea', of what he wants to say, the first stage would be for the phrase structure rules of the syntactic component to generate deep structures for input to the semantic component until it produces a semantic representation which matches the semantic 'idea'. At the next stage the transformational component could come directly into action to map the selected deep structure on to a surface structure. This would then be fed into the phonological component so as to produce the actual sounds of the sentence.

At first sight it might appear that, on the basis of this model, speech production is more plausibly accounted for than speech perception. Once a correct deep structure has been found to match the semantic representation of the 'idea', the rest of the generative process can occur in the direction in which the rules are specified in the grammar. On the incoming side the synthesizing process has to begin right from the deep structure level in order even to set about assigning a matching surface structure. However, the whole analysis-by-synthesis notion is in itself highly counter-intuitive. The idea that a person arrives at a match either for 'what he wants to say' or for a sequence of incoming sounds by allowing his knowledge of syntactic rules to start generating strings at random would obviously be wildly uneconomical. When one thinks of all the possible deep structure frameworks coupled with all the possible words that might be inserted from the lexicon, it would clearly take an unmanageable amount of time before the correct matching string happened to be produced. Indeed, strictly speaking, since the grammar is supposed to be capable of generating an infinite number of strings, it is theoretically possible that the matching string would *never* be produced. All that Katz and Postal say about this is to suggest that there must be some heuristic devices for cutting down the number of strings that would need to be generated each time. These would presumably allow for such factors as the phonetic sounds of the incoming string helping to determine which items are selected from the lexicon or, equivalently on the production side, choice of lexical items with appropriate semantic features to match the speaker's 'idea'. However, there are no indications about how such procedures could be incorporated into the model.

Nevertheless, the value of Katz and Postal's model is that, by adhering so strictly to the rules prescribed in transformational grammar, it brings to light difficulties that might have been overlooked in a more loosely formulated model. In particular it highlights the problem of how to allow for speakers' options within the framework of a generative grammar designed to generate all possible sentences on an essentially random basis. The implausibility of the analysis-by-synthesis model makes it clear that a speaker must have the ability to make use of his knowledge of the language to select rules that are appropriate to the pattern of incoming sounds or are under the control of his semantic intentions. This interaction of different levels of analysis in sentence processing makes it difficult to maintain the assumption that a full syntactic analysis is carried out prior to and independently of semantic analysis. The approach to be described in the next section is concerned with the way in which a variety of cues other than formal transformations may interact in perception of sentence meaning.

Non-transformational deep structure models

An example of a model based on the proposition that speech perception may not depend solely on the use of transformational rules is presented in an article by Fodor and Garrett (1967). While agreeing that the process of understanding a sentence is concerned with recovering its deep structure relations, they argue that this is essentially a perceptual process. Consequently, the important factor is not the number of transformational steps specified by the grammar for generating the sentence but rather 'the degree to which the arrangement of elements in the surface structure provides clues to the relations of elements in deep structure'. However, since in general the greater the number of transformations the more likely surface structure is to be distorted from deep structure, thus tending to obliterate clues to deep structure relations, predictions based on transformational and perceptual complexity tend to run in the same direction. Examples quoted by Fodor and Garrett where this is not the case include an adjective noun phrase like *the red house*, which requires extra transformations to derive it from *the house which is red*, and yet gives a clearer perceptual cue to the deep structure relation between *red* and *house*. Similarly, the dropping of the agent from a passive requires an extra transformation and yet the shorter passive, e.g. *The boy was bitten* as against *The boy was bitten by the man* appears to be less perceptually complex.

In order to test their theory Fodor and Garrett carried out an experiment in which they investigated comprehension of embedded sentences as a function of whether they included relative pronouns or not. They found that sentences like *The shot (which) the soldier (that) the mosquito bit fired missed* were more difficult to paraphrase when the pronouns were left out than when they were included. This was interpreted as evidence in support of the hypothesis that the pronouns were providing perceptual cues about deep structure relations between the subjects and objects of the embedded clauses. As a control for the possibility that the difficulty of the non-pronoun sentences could be put down to the extra transformations needed to delete them, Fodor and Garrett also demonstrated that the addition of adjectives, which would theoretically entail several extra transformations, had no adverse effect. On the contrary the sentence *The first shot the tired soldier the mosquito bit fired missed* was actually easier than the version without adjectives. This seems odd since, regardless of the means by which deep structure is extracted, the sentence with adjectives must have a more complex deep structure than the sentence without adjectives. Perhaps the adjectives acted as extra cues which helped to separate or identify the nouns, or they may have been ignored in the experimental task of sorting out subject and object relations. In either case the experiment demonstrates the lack of a one-to-one correspondence between number of transformations linking deep and surface structure and perceptual complexity.

Fodor and Garrett argue from this that, rather than attempting to undo grammatical transformations, subjects use their knowledge of likely deep structures cued by surface structure features. One example of such a perceptual mapping rule (so termed by Bever, 1970) would be that two nouns following each other at the beginning of a sentence might be a clue to the deep structure underlying a sentence such as *The boy the girl and the man left and walked down the road*. The presence of a relative pronoun as in *The boy whom the girl left and the man walked down the road* rules out the possibility of this deep structure analysis. However, the authors go on to point out that even in this second case one cannot always apply the rule that the second noun *girl* is the subject of an action involving the first noun *boy* as its object. This rule depends on choice of verb since there are cases such as *The boy whom the girl wanted the man to meet* in which *the boy* is not the direct object of *the girl wanted*.

The conclusion they draw is that the complexity of a sentence is a direct function of the number of possible deep structure relations the lexical items can enter into. Thus, if one hears the sequence of words *The boy whom the girl left* there is only one possible deep structure subject and object relation between *the boy* and *the girl* because *left* is a transitive verb. On the other hand, because the verb *wanted* has two syntactic functions, the sequence *The boy whom the girl wanted* would allow more than one possible relationship between *the boy* and *the girl*, depending on the rest of the sentence.

Fodor, Garrett and Bever (1968) carried out an ingenious experiment in which they showed that sentences with verbs that are compatible with only one deep structure are easier than sentences with structurally ambiguous verbs. For instance, in a task involving construction of sentences out of scrambled words, the sentence *The man whom the child met carried a box* was easier than *The man whom the child knew carried a box*. The potential deep structure ambiguity of the latter sentence arises from the fact that the verb *knew* is also compatible with a sentence such as *The man whom the child knew carried a box was dangerous*.

This type of analysis has two implications. The first is that knowledge of the deep structure relations into which a word can enter, which is thought of as being stored in the lexicon, interacts with surface structure cues in the perception of sentences. This is further evidence against the strict transformational hypothesis that the sets of operations involved at each level of linguistic analysis are independent of one another. The second, and perhaps even more crucial, implication is that people start processing incoming sounds as soon as they hear them. On the perception side, just as with sentence production, language users have options open to them of possible deep structure interpretations as a sentence unfolds. Transformational grammar, on the other hand, is founded on the notion that sentences can be analysed only in terms of their overall structure.

One consequence of this way of looking at speech perception is to have redirected attention to the left-to-right constraints affecting the production and perception of sentences. Since linguists work with complete sentences, they can formulate their analysis of top-to-bottom structure in the way most convenient for their purpose, disregarding the temporal order in which words actually appear. The language user, on the other hand, has to base his analysis on the words as they are presented one by one and, as shown in the above experiments, this may affect his perception of overall structure. Interest in this aspect of language has naturally led to a greater concern with surface structure which, unlike deep structure, reflects the order of words as they occur in a sentence. The surface structure models described in the next sections are motivated by this consideration.

Surface structure models: Yngve's theory

Models of language based solely on the surface structure of sentences are contrary to Chomsky's transformational grammar in that they reject the need for deep structure analysis, either as a means of expressing underlying syntactic regularities or as a necessary prerequisite for semantic interpretation. The reasons for including them here are twofold. First, there is the theoretical point mentioned at the end of the last section. As is repeatedly emphasized in Chomsky's theory, the ordering of elements in deep structure may be quite different from that of the words in the final sentence, since deep structure analysis is designed to express just those basic subject and object relations that are often distorted in surface structure. But in natural language use words are produced or perceived in a left-to-right order corresponding to surface structure order.

The other major interest of the surface structure approach is that, because of its concentration on just the one level of surface form, it appears to have more in common with psychologists' traditional interest in verbal behaviour. The influence of structural factors is considerably more acceptable if the structure concerned is clearly derived from the actual stimulus presented; in other words the surface order of words in a sentence rather than some abstract deep structure at many removes from manifest language. Nevertheless, it is interesting that, in spite of its apparently simpler one-level analysis, surface structure theory runs into many of the same conceptual difficulties as models based on transformational grammar.

Before going on to discuss these, there is one point that needs to be clarified in advance. Surface structure models are also known as phrase structure models because they are formulated as hierarchies of immediate constituents of the kind that can be generated by phrase structure rewriting rules. As pointed out in the discussion on pages 78–80, these phrase structure rules have the same form as those used by Chomsky to generate deep structure strings. However, although for convenience of exposition Chomsky's phrase structure rewriting rules are often shown as generating actual sentences, the crucial difference is that in Chomsky's theory the role of phrase structure rules is confined to generating underlying deep structures. This distinction becomes obvious as soon as the grammar is applied to more complex sentences, the deep structures for which will consist of a series of kernel strings that have to undergo many transformations in order to turn them into their final surface form. Chomsky is thus totally opposed to the idea that surface structure can be directly generated by phrase structure rules. Moreover, while the final surface structure of a sentence may also take the form of a tree diagram of constituent units, Chomsky maintains that such an analysis, while required for phonological representation, reveals none of the underlying syntactic relations needed for semantic interpretation.

The opposite view that it is the surface structure of a sentence that determines language performance is represented in its most theoretical form in Yngve's model of language. Nevertheless, in some ways the formulation of the model, which Yngve presented to the American Philosophical Society in 1960, and more informally in *Scientific American* in 1962, bears interesting resemblances to Chomsky's theory. Just as the aim of transformational grammar is to provide a formal set of rules which could be run through by a machine in order to produce the sentences of a language, Yngve's system takes the form of a computer program for generating sentences for the purpose of machine translation. The program instructions are binary rewrite rules which sub-divide symbols into further symbols, at the end rewriting symbols as words (see the simplified example given in Figure 12). In order to cope with complex sentences, sophisticated rules are included which, for instance, allow for discontinuous constituents, which had always proved a difficult problem for straightforward constituent analysis. Figure 12 shows Yngve's ingenious proposal for generating a verb and its complement when they do not come together in a sentence. In this case the verb phrase constituent *makes black* is generated as one unit, which is then rewritten as verb and verb complement; but by use of the dashed line the two constituents occur separated by *it* in the actual sentence. The reason for generating *makes black* as a single unit is presumably because it occurs as such in other sentences like *The kettle was made black by the steam*.

Other features of the program allow for the selection of Passive instead of Simple Sentence which results in a different set of rewriting rules coming into operation. The recursive aspect of language is catered for by allowing symbols to re-occur in the rewriting of later symbols, as in the simplified example given in Figure 13 which could obviously be extended infinitely.

However, if Yngve's system merely consisted of an alternative set of rules for generating an infinite number of sentences, it would not be of much interest to psychologists. Yngve

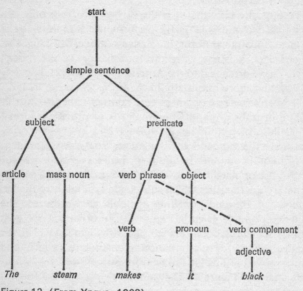

Figure 12   (From Yngve, 1962)

admits in his 1962 article that the rules as then presented could generate only the first ten sentences in a well-known children's book. Moreover, in the course of doing this the program also produced many meaningless sentences, presumably because not enough selection restrictions had been written in to prevent anomalous combinations of words. An even more important point is that Yngve's system offers no way of expressing intuitive relationships between actives, passives, negatives and so on, since according to the rules these are derived quite independently. Nor can the rules account for underlying ambiguities, being concerned only with generating the surface structure of phrases like *The shooting of the hunters*.

Where Yngve scores is that, because he actually puts his program to work to produce sentences, he comes up against two constraints that are ignored by the rules of transformational grammar. The first is that he has to take into account what the computer has to store in order to carry out the program. Secondly, the aim of the program is to get the computer to print out the words of the sentence in their final left-to-right

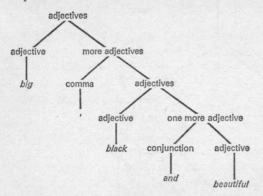

Figure 13 (From Yngve, 1962)

order. With Chomsky's rules, as long as higher level branches are rewritten before lower level branches that depend on them, there is no restriction on the order in which the symbols of a sentence are produced; for instance, it does not in general matter whether the subject NP or the predicate VP is generated first.

Yngve's method for dealing with these points is as follows. Assuming that the set of rewriting rules is stored in the computer's long term memory, the program starts with the initial symbol and continues rewriting symbols, following each *left hand* branch until it arrives at the first word. While it is doing this it has to store in short term memory any other symbols that are going to need further generation. In Figure 14 this would mean that, by the time the computer had printed out the word *The*, it would be holding in store the symbol Predicate as a result of its first rewriting division of Simple Sentence into Subject and Predicate, and the symbol Mass Noun as a result of the division of Subject into Article and Mass Noun. The next step would be to go back to the last symbol stored in short term memory, in this case mass noun as shown by the dotted arrow, and rewrite it as *steam*.

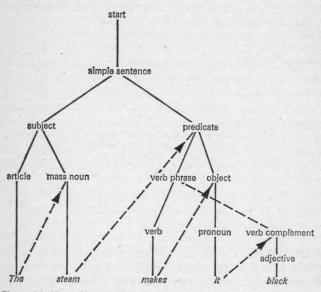

Figure 14 (From Yngve. 1962)

As no new symbols would have to be entered into short term memory during the generation of Mass Noun as *steam*, the program goes back to Predicate and continues down left hand branches until it reaches the word *makes*. At this point it will be keeping in short term store first the symbol Object as a result of dividing Predicate into Verb Phrase and Object, and later the 'postponed' discontinuous constituent Verb Complement, resulting from the rewriting of Verb Phrase as

Verb and Verb Complement. Whereas the normal procedure would be to go back to Verb Complement since it was the last symbol to be entered into short term memory, because of the postponement the program proceeds as shown by the dotted arrow to Object. Only after having printed out the word *it* does it go back to finish the generation of Verb Complement to produce the word *black*. The aim of this whole procedure is to generate the words of the sentence in their final left-to-right order within the framework of the overall syntactic structure of the sentence.

The most important implication of Yngve's model is that as each word is produced there are certain commitments in terms of the number of symbol items that have to be stored in short term memory for future generation. In the example in Figure 14 at the point of producing *The* there are two items in memory (Predicate and Mass Noun), at *steam* just one item (Predicate), at *makes* two items (Object and Verb Complement), at *it* one item (Verb Complement) and at *black* no items. These numbers of stored items are what Yngve calls the 'depth' of a word. The point he is making is that for any device with a finite memory there must be a limit to the number of items that can be stored at any one time. For human beings Yngve suggests that a plausible limit would be around seven items, which accords with the average memory span of items that a person can repeat back or remember for a short time, as with a telephone number (for further details see George Miller's well-known article on the 'magical number 7' (1956)). From this it would follow that any sentence which requires storage of more than seven symbols while a word is being produced would be beyond the capacity of a language user. This measure of the largest number of items that have to be stored at any one time Yngve terms the 'maximum depth' of a sentence.

The kind of constructions that lead to greater or lesser depth depend on whether sentences branch more to the left or to the right, the former resulting in more items having to be kept in store. For example, the sentence in Figure 15 has a maximum depth of 4 as compared to 3 for the sentence in Figure 16, as shown by the bracketed depth numbers indicating the number of symbols that have to be stored as each word is produced. The reader may like to verify that with a system of binary divisions – and when there are no discontinuous constituents – the depth number for each word can be calculated by counting the number of *left* branches involved in its generation.

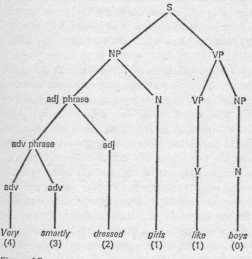

Figure 15

Yngve goes on to a very interesting discussion of the sort of linguistic devices made use of in English in order to reduce depth. Moving left branching constructions from the beginning of a sentence to the end is one method of achieving this, as shown in Figures 15 and 16. One particularly interesting point about this example is that it is the more complex passive sentence that has the lower depth, suggesting that depth reduction is one of the stylistic considerations involved in selection of the passive. Yngve gives many other examples of constructions which can be used to reduce depth, as, for instance, optional ordering of direct and indirect object to select a sentence like *He gave the candy to the girl that he met in New York while visiting his parents for ten days around Christmas and New Year* in preference to *He gave the girl that he met in New York while visiting his parents for ten days around Christmas and New Year the candy.* Yngve claims that many of the apparently arbitrary and unnecessarily complicated stylistic options available in English become much more explicable if looked at in the light of their role in depth reduction.

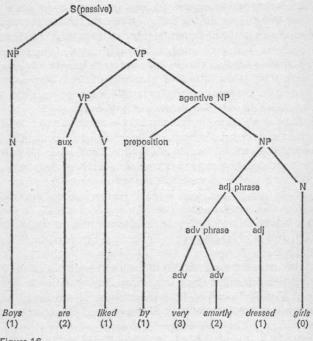

Figure 16

From the point of view of providing a model of speech production, Yngve's theory has the further advantage that it does not assume that a speaker has to have prior knowledge of the total overall structure of the final sentence. The idea is that when the first word is produced all that needs to be stored is the minimum number of items necessary to complete an English sentence. Looking back to figure 14, after uttering the word *The* there must follow at least a noun and a predicate. But after the noun *steam* the sentence could be completed with just a one word predicate such as *hisses*. In the case of the next word *makes* the position is slightly more complicated since in the course of generating it the speaker must be presumed to know that *makes* is functioning as a transitive verb with a verb complement and so requires at least two more words such as *it* and *black*. However, the basic notion is that the speaker only needs to know the minimum number of items needed to finish a sentence, without having to take into account the way in which these items will finally turn out to be rewritten at lower levels. This is an attractive proposition which appears to account for the speaker's ability to follow up options and add new elaborations to his utterance as he goes along.

Equally plausible, too, is the implication that the listener, through his own knowledge of the rewriting rules, builds up expectancies about forthcoming units. Thus, when he hears the word *The*, he knows that it must be followed by at least a noun and a verb to complete the sentence. As the sentence unfolds from left, to right he gains further information revising his expectancies about how the sentence is likely to end. In this way Yngve's theory appears to account for the left-to-right aspects of language behaviour in the case of both speaker and hearer.

However, there are certain difficulties about this model of language behaviour. For one thing, to what extent does 'depth' itself depend on knowledge of overall structure? For instance, a sentence such as *Boys are liked by very smartly dressed girls* would be allotted the depth numbers shown in figure 16. But how plausible is this as a representation of the speaker's or hearer's options assuming that they are not already aware of the final form of the whole sentence? It may seem reasonable enough that the speaker as he utters the word *are* would know that he had already selected a passive option, and had thus committed himself to production of a verb and an agentive noun phrase. However, when he comes to the

word *liked*, shouldn't he be committed to at least two more
words to produce a minimal agentive noun phrase such as *by
girls*? But the depth number of (1) for *liked* does not reflect the
speaker's knowledge that an agentive phrase must consist of at
least two words. When one considers the listener the position
is even more problematical. As the sentence unfolds there is no
reason to suppose that it is not going to be completed as, say,
Boys are ugly, in which case at the point when the listener hears
are he might be expecting only one more word to follow. In
this connection, it is interesting that Martin and Roberts
(1966), who carried out the first experiments testing Yngve's
depth hypothesis, stress the point that intonation in terms of
pitch and stress may give cues to the listener about the number
of words still to come.

This problem of depth expectancies is, however, circum-
vented by Martin and Robert's use of a sentence recall paradigm. In a memory experiment, just as the experimenter can
base his calculation of depth numbers on the already known
overall structure of the sentences to be presented, so the subject can wait until he hears the whole sentence before storing
it in memory. And when he comes to recall it he is attempting
to reproduce his already stored codings rather than taking up
the options available when generating a new sentence.

Leaving aside for the moment the question of whether this
reflects the normal behaviour of speaker or listener, Martin
and Roberts go on to hypothesize that the more memory
commitments involved in the structure of a sentence, the more
difficult it will be to recall. One interesting point is that the
measure of depth used in these experiments is based neither on
Yngve's maximum depth, nor on the total number of items
stored in memory during the production of a sentence. Instead
Martin and Roberts take the *mean* of the depth numbers
attached to the words in a sentence. For example, the mean
depth of the sentence in Figure 15 would be the sum of the
word depth numbers (11) divided by the number of words in
the sentence (6), i.e. 1.83. That for the sentence in Figure 16
would come out as 11 divided by 8, i.e. 1.38.

An obvious advantage of this measure is that it controls

sentence length when calculating structural complexity. But this leads to the rather curious situation that length of sentence would not in itself be expected to affect recall performance. An extreme example would be a very long but right branching sentence, in which future commitments at any one point are minimal giving a low mean depth, and yet the sentence as a whole would impose a considerable burden on memory storage. In any case, Yngve's concentration on storage of *future* commitments ignores the fact that the memorizer has to keep track of all the units that have occurred earlier in the sentence.

In view of the above points, it is not surprising that in one of Martin and Robert's experiments (1967) in which sentence length was varied, it was shown to have a major effect on subjects' recall performance. However, in the crucial experiments in which Martin and Roberts compared the depth hypothesis against the transformational hypothesis, sentence length was in fact controlled. Using sentences seven words long they constructed sets of kernel, negative and passive sentences (including shortened passives without agents), so that each type of sentence had either a low mean depth or a high mean depth. Looking at subjects' recall performance Martin and Roberts found that mean depth was a more important factor than sentence type. Indeed, in so far as sentence type had any effect it was the surprising one of kernel sentences being *less* well recalled than more complex sentences. The authors argue that this throws considerable doubt on the transformational hypothesis; and go on to administer the *coup de grâce* by showing that the sentences used in an experiment by Mehler (1963), which was interpreted as demonstrating a recall effect due to transformational complexity, also differed in mean depth in the same direction, kernels having a depth of 1.17, passives 1.38, negatives 1.43 and passive negatives 1.67.

While this may seem conclusive evidence that storage of future commitments as measured by Yngve depth is the crucial factor affecting subjects' performance, the very fact that transformations tend to produce differential mean depths points to the difficulty of manipulating depth as an independent factor. In order to equate depth and sentence length it is necessary to add extra adjectives and adverbs to some of the active sentences. But this immediately raises the issue of whether one is thereby introducing other factors that might adversely affect recall performance. When Martin, Roberts and Collins (1968) looked at the variable of differential forgetting of word classes they found that some types of words such as adverbs and adjectives were less often recalled than nouns, verbs and objects. As a result, low depth actives, which required padding out with two extra adjectives, were recalled less frequently than low depth passives, which had only one extra adjective.

Another way of looking at this is to say that predictions based on transformational theory can be expected to hold only when the transformed sentences are related to the same 'kernel' semantic content. Consequently, it is not surprising that addition of extra adjectives and adverbs might offset any differences due to transformational complexity. Equally, since Martin and Roberts used quite different sentences for the various depth and sentence type combinations, there is no guarantee that high and low depth sentences were equated for semantic content.

In an attempt to control for this factor of equal semantic content, Wright (1969) used sentences in which depth was manipulated by moving relative clauses towards the beginning or end of a sentence. Examples of a pair of active sentences are:

The guard who was looking through the window watched the prisoner

and

The guard watched the prisoner who was looking through the window

The first of these sentences has a considerably higher mean depth than the second, while the semantic content is virtually identical. Equivalent passive sentences were also used and memory storage was measured by the Savin and Perchonock method (see p. 111 for an account of this procedure). Wright's results showed no differences between the high and low depth versions of each pair of sentences for which sentence length, sentence type and semantic content were constant. The greater difficulty of the passives over the actives, regardless of depth, could be put down to the fact that the passive sentences were slightly longer or, possibly, to semantic factors such as confusion about whether the relative clause was attached to the subject or object of the sentence, as in *The prisoner who was looking through the window was watched by the guard.*

Rather than keeping semantic content constant, an experiment by Perfetti (1969) tackled the same issue by investigating the effect of varying amount of semantic content independently of depth. As an index of semantic content he calculated the ratio of lexical words to grammatical words in a sentence. This measure of what he calls *lexical density* is based on a commonly accepted linguistic distinction between open and closed classes of words. The class of *lexical* words is termed open because it includes word classes such as nouns, adjectives, verbs and adverbs, to which new words can be added virtually without limit. *Grammatical* words refer to classes of articles, pronouns, auxiliaries, and so on, which are closed in the sense that each language has a limited set. The distinction is roughly equivalent to that often made between content and function words. Perfetti used ten-word long sentences, which were of four types: low lexical density (i.e. 5 lexical words – those not in italics) and low depth, e.g. *The* family *has* accepted *an* offer *to* purchase *the* house; low lexical density and high depth, e.g. *The* use *of* credit *by the* consumer *has* obviously increased; high lexical density (7 lexical words) and low depth, e.g. *The* police watched nearly every move *of the* clever thief; and high lexical density and high depth, e.g. *The* almost never used machine *is* too expensive *to* keep.

Perfetti's results showed that the only factor affecting recall was lexical density, there being no differences between sentences due to variations in mean depth. Discussing these findings the author makes the point that the difficulty of sentences with more lexical words might be due to the greater choice of open class words, making them more unpredictable and thus more difficult to remember. A particularly interesting, and not unrelated, suggestion is that another aspect of high lexical density sentences is that they would tend to have more complex deep structures. The reason for this is that, given that sentences are of equal length, as they were in this case, the only way in which a deep structure consisting of more embedded strings can be accommodated is by deleting as many as possible of the connecting words joining these strings together. An example may help to clarify this point. In deep structure, modification of nouns by adjectives is handled by extra embedded subordinate strings. Thus, *The gay red hat* can be thought of as involving two strings in deep structure: *The hat is red* and *The hat is gay*. Intermediate stages would be *The hat which is red is gay* and *The red hat is gay*, finally producing *The gay red hat*. The point is that each of these versions involves dropping grammatical words, arriving at the shortest version *The gay red hat* with the highest proportion of lexical words. What it comes down to is that, if semantic complexity depends on the number of embedded strings in deep structure, the amount of semantic content that can be crammed into a sentence of a given length will be maximized by the number of deletion and contraction transformations that have been put into effect. To the extent that the deleted words can be left out without affecting semantic content, they could be said to be redundant in the sense of being predictable in a given syntactic framework.

Perfetti's results once again confirm the pre-eminence of semantic factors in sentence processing. It is particularly interesting, too, that, as soon as semantic content is taken into account, notions about deep and surface structure begin to creep in again. However, since deep structure is often expressed in a form that does not correspond to surface word order, this still leaves the problem of how semantic content is related to the final left-to-right sequence of words in a sentence. The next section will be devoted to N. F. Johnson's theory, which is specifically concerned with left-to-right dependencies exhibited in subjects' recall of sentences as a function of how they store surface structure units.

Surface structure models: Johnson's theory

Johnson's model (1965, 1966a, b, 1969) is similar to those based on the depth hypothesis in that it assumes that subjects store sentences in the form that will be needed for recall output. Moreover, he accepts that the process of generating a sentence for recall is carried out according to Yngve's rewriting operations. However, rather than looking at future commitments incurred during sentence production, Johnson concentrates on the actual response units into which a sentence is organized for subsequent recall.

Taking as his starting point the simplest S–R position, Johnson considers the possibility that subjects might be learning sentences as lists of isolated words, forming associations between each item and the next to build up a chain of responses in which each word acts as a stimulus to the next. Other psychologists, however, have suggested that, rather than learning lists by a succession of equally weighted S – R associations, subjects recode the material into larger units, or 'chunks' to use George Miller's term, which serve to reduce the items that have to be remembered to a number that is within short term memory capacity.

In order to investigate these two possibilities, Johnson devised a measure of the degree of association between adjacent words during recall, the point of which is to show whether the successive words in a sentence are all equally strongly associated, or whether they are grouped together into 'chunks' of highly associated words. The argument is that, if there is a strong S – R association between two adjacent words, then if the first is recalled correctly this should lead to correct recall of the second as well. But, if the two items are not highly associated, there is no special likelihood that correct recall of the first should result in correct recall of the second. Johnson's measure calculates the conditional probability of a word being recalled incorrectly given that the preceding word is correct. Divided by the number of times that the first word is itself recalled correctly, this gives the proportion of transitional errors that occur between any two words, or transitional error probability (TEP). The higher this probability of making a transitional error, the *less* association there is presumed to be between any adjacent pair of words. Such a measure thus gives an indication of whether some groups of words are more closely associated together than others.

Using this measure on subjects' recall of sentences, Johnson found that TEPs were not spread out evenly between each succeeding pair of words, as might be expected if associations between adjacent words form the basis for learning. Instead, higher TEPs were found between pairs of words occurring at the breaks between major surface structure constituents. For example, with a sentence like *The tall boy saved the dying woman* (see Figure 17), the highest proportion of transitional errors occurred between *boy* and *saved*, that is, at the break between subject and predicate. In sentences like *The house across the street is burning* the highest TEPs were between *house* and *across* and between *street* and *is*, corresponding to a surface structure analysis into three constituents *The house – across the street – is burning*.

From this evidence that word to word associations are *less* strong across boundaries between major constituents, Johnson argues that surface structure analysis acts as a recoding scheme for organizing the words in a sentence into a small number of recall units, which are equivalent to the major constituents of the sentence. His suggestion is that these highly associated response units are remembered as a whole. Thus, with a phrase like *the dying woman*, which is likely to be coded as one unit, having got *the* correct there is a low probability of making a transitional error on *dying* and *woman*. In contrast, when a word to word transition occurs at a break between the last word of one unit and the first word of the next, as between *boy* and *saved*, there is a high probability of a transitional error on *saved* in spite of getting *boy* correct, since *boy* and *saved* do not form part of one constituent unit.

A strong implication of the proposition that response units are remembered as a whole is that either all the words in a major constituent should be perfectly recalled or none at all. However, Johnson found that some transitional errors occurred even within constituent units, and further that these were not equally distributed between pairs of words in a major unit. In order to account for this finding, Johnson makes the plausible suggestion that sentences consist of a hierarchy of constituent units and sub-units, transitional error probability being a function of the level at which a transition from unit to unit occurs. To take an example, in the sentence in Figure 17 the break between the pair of adjacent words *boy* and *saved* represents a high level transition from subject to predicate.

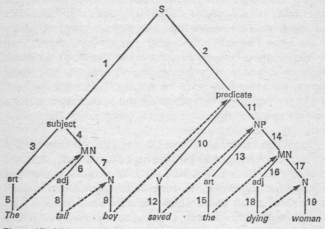

Figure 17 (Adapted from Johnson, 1966a)

However, within the predicate the transition from V to NP between the words *saved* and *the*, although less major than that between *boy* and *saved*, is in its turn at a higher level than that between *dying* and *woman*. Assuming that the lower the level of a word to word transition, the more closely a pair of words will be associated, this would lead one to expect a hierarchy of TEPs, highest at breaks between major constituents and progressively lower at transitions between minor constituents.

The next question to be considered is how to measure the level at which breaks between major and minor constituents occur. Because of his concern with coding of sentences into 'chunks' that will be recalled as complete response units, Johnson uses as his measure of transition level the number of rewriting operations needed to decode the whole of the unit following each break. The rationale is that, since a unit will be stored in memory as a whole, it must be fully decoded before it will be produced at all.

As can be seen in Figure 17, these rewriting operations are virtually identical to those in Yngve's model. Thus the first step is to rewrite S as subject and predicate (operations 1 & 2), the next to store predicate in short term memory while rewriting subject as art and MN – modified noun (operations 3 & 4), then storing MN while rewriting art as *The* (operation 5). As in Yngve's model, the next stage is to backtrack to the symbol most recently stored, in this case, as shown by the dotted arrow, MN, which is then rewritten as adj and N (operations 6 & 7). The symbol N is then stored during the rewriting of adj as *tall* (operation 8) and then itself rewritten as *boy* (operation 9). It is only at this stage that the decoder returns to predicate and continues to rewrite symbols in the order shown by the numbered operations.

In order to calculate the number of operations involved at each word to word transition, Johnson counts the operations needed to decode the whole of the unit beginning with the second word. Thus, at the transition between *The* and *tall* the next unit is the MN *tall boy* which requires four operations to decode (operations 6, 7, 8 & 9). The transition between *tall* and *boy* requires only the one operation to decode N into *boy* (operation 9). But moving to the transition between *boy* and *saved*, the next unit beginning with *saved* is the whole predicate which needs a total of 10 operations to decode (operations 10 to 19). The transition between *saved* and *the* requires the seven operations needed to decode the NP *the dying woman* (operations 13 to 19); that between *the* and *dying* four operations (16 to 19); and that between *dying* and *woman* just one operation (19).

When comparing this analysis with Yngve's, one obvious difference is that Yngve's model leaves a degree of uncertainty as to how the rest of a sentence is to be completed. Thus, in

Figure 17, after predicate has been rewritten as V and NP, while V is being rewritten as *saved* NP is kept in store; and could theoretically be rewritten as any noun phrase, producing, for instance, *The tall boy saved the elephant*. In contrast, for the purpose of predicting TEPs Johnson assumes that a person must know how to decode the predicate into all its constituent words before he will produce even the first word *saved*. This leads to certain logical difficulties. For one thing, it means that the operations needed to decode sub-units are counted more than once. Thus at the transition from *boy* to *saved*, instead of counting just the operations needed to produce the word *saved* (operations 10 to 12), as would be expected according to the Yngve model, Johnson counts the total number of operations needed for the whole unit (operations 10 to 19). But when it comes to the next transition between *saved* and *the*, all the operations needed to produce *the dying woman* (operations 13 to 19) have to be repeated, and so on for the rest of the words in the predicate. The point is that, if it is true that the subject will not produce the first word of the predicate unless he can decode it as a whole into the words *saved the dying woman*, then it seems superfluous for him to have to return to higher level units and repeat these decoding operations. To carry this argument to its extreme, shouldn't the subject refuse to produce any words at all unless he remembers the decoding operations for the whole sentence? Somewhat inconsistently, when he is calculating the operations involved in producing the *first* word of a sentence, Johnson follows the Yngve practice of counting only operations 1 to 5, predicate and MN being left undecoded. But, according to Johnson's usual method of calculation, how could the first word *The* be produced unless a person has available at least operations 1 to 9 needed for decoding the subject unit *The tall boy* as a whole? Johnson's theory thus seems to be an uneasy mixture between a recall model, based on the idea of organizing a sentence into a series of fully precoded chunks, and a production model based on Yngve's notion of the speaker producing one word at a time, keeping higher level units in storage to be decoded at a later stage.

The above discussion highlights some of what one might call the technical difficulties involved in characterizing surface structure operations. An even more serious problem is the possibility that subjects are responding to other levels of analysis. For instance, one particularly awkward factor for a theory based on word to word transitions is that grammatical constraints do not operate only between adjacent words in a sentence. Thus, a set of sentences taken from one of Johnson's experiments included the following:

The house across the street is burning
The men who left early are listening
The dogs with black tails are running
The child who sings well was found
The fish from the lake are cooking

Clearly, remembering whether the subject is singular or plural will determine the number of the main verb, although this relationship will not be reflected in Johnson's measure of transitional error probability between pairs of adjacent words.

Looking, too, at the possible effect of semantic cues, it seems obvious that in the above sentences there are differential degrees of probability that subjects, dependent clauses and predicates might be freely interchanged or are likely to go together. This sort of consideration might in itself account for the finding that major constituents tend to be remembered as wholes. The possibility that semantic congruency is an important factor is also borne out by another finding reported by Johnson, that there is a special tendency for 'inessential' adjectives and adverbs to be deleted or remembered incorrectly regardless of whether they occur at a major break in the sentence or not. Because of this, in a recent paper (1969) Johnson makes the point that his model only predicts what he calls 'stop errors', i.e. when a correct word is followed by a complete blank representing a failure to recall the next response unit as a whole. However, not only does this leave in abeyance the question of what factors do cause deletion, substitution and other types of errors, but it has also been shown that, when subjects are given a longer time to recall the sentences than the few seconds allowed by Johnson, this leads to a virtual elimination of stop errors and a different TEP pattern (Langford, in preparation).

What this amounts to is an admission that the effect of semantic factors cannot be handled within Johnson's model based on surface structure rewriting operations. It was exactly this same problem that led George Miller to abandon the attempt to explain performance as a function of transformational complexity. This crucial question of the relation between syntactic rules and semantic content will be taken up again in the next section in the course of discussing the advantages and disadvantages of deep structure and surface structure models of language use.

Deep structure versus surface structure

Clearly, it is the proponents of surface structure models who have parsimony on their side. Not only do such models take into account only *one* level of analysis; but this is the common-sense level concerned with the left-to-right order of words in sentences as they are actually uttered or heard. It is a fair point that it is up to the supporters of transformational models to demonstrate the necessity for introducing an extra, and unobservable, level of underlying deep structure.

The arguments for deep structure fall into two groups. One line of approach is experimental evidence to show that subjects' performance in linguistic tasks cannot be fully explained by surface structure considerations. Especially relevant to Johnson's theory about recoding of sentences into constituent units is some research carried out by Bever and others investigating the linguistic units with which people operate. The technique was to introduce a click into one ear while subjects were listening to a sentence in the other and ask them to report at what point in the sentence they thought the click had occurred. Having found (Fodor and Bever, 1965) that the click tended to be displaced from its objective position either backwards or forwards to the nearest break between major constituent units, Bever (1971) went on to use the technique with sentences in which the breaks between deep and surface structure units do not necessarily coincide. In these experiments the deep structure organization of sentences was shown to have a definite effect on click location even when differences in deep structure were not reflected in surface structure.

Another interesting way of looking at the structural organization of sentences has been developed by Levelt (1970). His method was unusually direct in that he simply asked subjects to make judgements about degrees of syntactic relatedness between pairs of words in sentences. Using a heirarchical clustering technique (Johnson S.C., 1967) for analysing the data, Levelt found that judgments about relatedness were a function of the phrase structure of a sentence. The lower the level of the unit the closer a pair of words are seen to be related. In Figure 17, for instance, one would expect to find *tall* and *boy* judged as more closely related than *boy* and *saved* which are only combined in a unit at the level of the whole sentence. This analysis fits in well with surface structure models. However, Levelt goes on to show that, when dealing with sentences in which not all deep structure relations are reflected in surface structure, deep structure still has an effect on subjects' judgements. An example he gives is the sentence *Carla takes the book and goes to school* (a translation of the Dutch sentence Levelt gave his Dutch subjects). In deep structure this would be analysed as two strings: *Carla takes the book* and *Carla goes to school*. Judgements by Levelt's subjects showed that they considered *Carla* and *goes* to be as closely related as *Carla* and *takes*, in spite of the fact that in the surface structure of the sentence *Carla* appears in close relationship only with *takes*.

The interesting point about this is the demonstration that syntactic associations can operate between words that are not adjacent to each other in surface structure. As pointed out earlier, this would be difficult to handle under a model such as Johnson's which relies solely on left-to-right associations between adjacent words. In this connection it would obviously be of interest to try out Johnson's measure of transitional error probability on sentences such as the 'Carla' one. For instance, would there be a higher probability of remembering *goes* given that one had recalled *Carla* or, alternatively, given that one had recalled the immediately preceding word *and*. Certainly, the work of both Bever and Levelt indicates that subjects are responding to underlying deep structure relations which have to be extracted from the immediately obvious surface form of a sentence.

The second line of defence for the psychological reality of deep structure rests on theoretical grounds, the main argument being the linguistic impossibility of accounting for the way in which people understand relations between sentences solely in terms of surface structure. There are sentences which can be assigned different meanings although they have only one surface structure, as in *The shooting of the hunters was awful*, and sentences which are seen as related despite having radically different surface structures, such as *The boy liked the girl* and *The girl was liked by the boy*. Or to take another example, Yngve's model would assign the same structure to the sentences *John is easy to please* and *John is eager to please*, thus ignoring the very different relationship between *John* and the verb *please* in the two sentences. Without an analysis of these underlying deep structure relations, not only would it be impossible to give a semantic interpretation to the two sentences, but there would be no explanation for the fact that it is permissible to say *It is easy to please John* but not *It is eager to please John*. This type of example is the basis for the Chomskyan contention that phrase structure analysis of surface structure is in principle incapable of accounting for a language user's understanding of his language.

The nub of the argument is that, as soon as syntactic analysis is thought of as providing information necessary for semantic interpretation, problems arise which are unresolvable at the surface structure level. In order to explain the language user's ability to resolve these ambiguities, it is necessary to involve a second level of deep structure. A further claim of Chomsky's theory is that transformational grammar gives the most economical and revealing analysis of the rules which map deep structure on to surface structure.

So far this line of argument has been pertinent to the weak

definition of competence, being concerned with which type of grammar gives the best description of linguistic usage, including the language user's intuitions about structural relations between sentences. The next question is whether transformational grammar fulfils the stronger definition of competence, by specifying the internalized knowledge of linguistic rules which enables a speaker to produce and understand sentences. At this point, it may be helpful to take the two main implications of Chomsky's theory separately: first, that the speaker must be aware of at least two levels of analysis, deep and surface structure; and, secondly, the claim that the rules which form the basis of the speaker's ability to map one level on to the other are transformational.

As far as the first of these propositions is concerned, the results from Bever and Levelt's research quoted at the beginning of this section indicate that, despite the initial plausibility of concentrating exclusively on the actual form of a sentence as uttered by speaker or heard by listener, subjects are also able to respond to a deeper level of syntactic analysis. Even more relevant is the plentiful evidence showing the effect of underlying semantic content on subject's performance. Since there can be no doubt that what a subject is actually exposed to is the surface form of a sentence, the crucial factor appears to be the *relation* between underlying semantic content and its expression in surface structure. In other words, the difficulty of a sentence cannot be explained by reference solely to either deep structure or surface structure, but is rather a function of the complexity of the connections between surface form and underlying semantic relations.

Making the crucial assumption, which will be taken up again later, that deep structure is an exact representation of semantic content, where does this leave the transformational hypothesis? In other words, do people make use of transformational and detransformational operations in order to get from deep structure to surface structure and vice versa? All the experimental evidence on this point tends *against* the notion that processing of sentences is a direct function of the number of transformational operations the grammar would assign for mapping deep on to surface structure. What seems to be a much more important factor is the presence of various cues in surface structure to underlying deep structure.

One type of cue that has been shown to have an effect is the information provided by lexical features of words. These may take the form of *syntactic* features indicating the kind of underlying relationships into which a verb can enter, as shown by Fodor et al.'s work (1968) with verbs like *know* which can occur in more than one kind of syntactic frame. Equally important are *semantic* features indicating, for instance, the likely relations between a lifeguard and a bather, as demonstrated in Slobin's and Herriot's experiments with non-reversible passives. It seems likely, too, that in Johnson's experiments subjects were making use of semantic cues when storing sentences for future recall. Research on Yngve's depth hypothesis also showed that more important than depth commitments were variations in the semantic content expressed in a sentence. For example, in the experiment reported by Wright, in which semantic content was held constant, depth had no effect; although presumably in extreme cases low or high depth versions of the same sentence content might result in deep structure relations being extracted more or less easily.

Further evidence concerning the importance of relationships between deep and surface structure comes from Perfetti's measure of lexical density. According to this, the more deep structure semantic content condensed into a sentence of a given length, the more difficult that sentence will be. The implication is that expressing the same amount of semantic content in a more diffuse surface form, while resulting in a longer sentence, would reduce the amount of lexical density. Finally, the experiments by Wason, Greene and Johnson-Laird (reported on page 116ff) show that choice of a particular transformational surface form for expressing the same semantic content can be made more or less easy to deal with according to the semantic function for which it is being used in that context, a result which goes directly against the notion that people always have to run through the same series of transformational operations when analysing the surface form of sentences.

It seems a fair conclusion from these experimental results that the number of transformational steps needed to get from deep to surface structure is not the major factor affecting the ease with which semantic content can be extracted from sentences. Subjects appear to rely more heavily on lexical and contextual cues, sometimes to the extent of by-passing syntactic analysis altogether, as when jumping to the wrong conclusion about what is happening in the 'unlikely' passive *The doctor is being treated by the patient*. Perhaps it is only in artificial situations when all such cues are denied them (as, for instance, in Trabasso's evaluation task in which subjects had to make hundreds of judgements about whether stimuli were *not orange* or *green*) that subjects resort to formal transformational and decision making operations.

To conclude this discussion of the strong claims of transformational grammar to describe the speaker's competence, it appears that the concepts of deep and surface structure are borne out as levels of analysis operative in language behaviour. But the hypothesis that transformational rules are used to relate these two levels cannot be accepted as an accurate account of the language user's ability to process sentences. A further implication is that sentence processing does not proceed as a series of independent analyses by the syntactic, semantic and phonological components, as prefigured in the 1965 version of Chomsky's theory. Instead, subjects seem to make use of cues at all different levels simultaneously, relying on a mixture of knowledge about possible deep structure relations, semantic information about word meanings and contextual cues.

At this point I should like to draw attention to one paradoxical feature of the psycholinguistic research cited in the above discussion. In spite of the fact that both Chomsky's transformational grammar and Yngve's surface structure model are expressed in the form of rewriting rules for *generating* sentences, virtually all these experiments have tested the effect of linguistic factors on subjects' *processing* of sentences; even in the case of sentence recall experiments the main interest has been in how subjects process sentences for storage. The discussion in the next section will, therefore, be concerned with the special problems involved in accounting for how a speaker goes about producing sentences.

Evaluation of speech production models

A strong underlying assumption of the psycholinguistic approach has been that speech perception is a mirror image of the processes involved in speech production; consequently, difficulties in perception are taken as a direct reflection of the operations taking place in speech production. Thus, demonstrations of perception or memory effects due to variables such as transformational complexity, Yngve depth or number of decoding operations have been treated as direct evidence that these same operations are carried out by the speaker when he produces sentences. Equally, negative evidence of the kind quoted in the previous section showing that people are not carrying out a detransformational analysis to process sentences tends to be interpreted as an argument against the use of transformations in speech production.

Certainly, it seems plausible enough that a speaker will be attempting to produce a sentence that his listener will find easy to understand (except perhaps in cases of deliberate mystification so often found in academic and other circles!). In strict logic, however, it does not necessarily follow that producing the version of a sentence easiest to assimilate by a listener should be the result of an equally simple process on the part of the speaker. As every writer, including the present author, knows only too well, success in expressing a complex idea in a surface form that makes it easy for the reader to extract the correct underlying semantic relations is likely to be the result of a great deal of effort put into choice of expression. For instance, it may be that extra transformations *are* needed to emphasize deep structure relations, as in the Fodor et al. example; or to postpone a phrase to the later part of a sentence in order to cut down memory storage as measured by Yngve depth; or to choose a 'natural' negative to express a contradiction in appropriate circumstances; or to reduce lexical density by expressing semantic content in a less condensed form, sometimes resulting in the need for a 'sentence division' transformation to divide an overlong sentence into more manageable units.

It is true that it does not seem likely that in ordinary conversation a speaker runs through a complicated set of transformations before he utters a sentence. Nevertheless, failure to find a one-to-one correspondence between number of transformations and subjects' *perceptual* performance does not necessarily rule out the possibility that the *speaker* has had to carry out those transformational operations in the first place.

The reason for the imbalance in the state of our knowledge about production and perception stems from the fact that in perception experiments the experimenter can to some extent mimic the 'real life' situation in which a listener is exposed to utterances which he has to interpret. As a result of being able to select the sentences to be presented to subjects, considerable advances have been made in investigating the factors affecting speech perception. In the case of speech production, on the other hand, there is the far more intractable problem of how the speaker himself chooses the semantic content which he wishes to convey and a surface form in which to express it.

When one looks at the various attempts that have been made to develop a model for speech production, it is clear that this question of the speaker's options is extremely difficult to handle within the framework of a generative grammar. This is due to the basic assumption that a grammar should consist of a system of formal rules which, if fed to a computer set to operate on a *random* basis, would be capable of generating all the sentences in a language. Both Chomsky's transformational grammar and Yngve's surface structure model face the problem of how to allow for a speaker's non-random choice of a particular sentence. It is important to bear this in mind when evaluating these two different formulations of grammatical rules against the requirements of a speech production model.

In specifying these requirements, we must again refer back to the distinction between competence and performance. According to the weaker definition of competence, a set of grammatical rules must meet the criterion of generating all permissible sentences and preventing the generation of non-grammatical utterances. On the stronger definition that the rules represent actual psychological operations, an explanation is needed of *how* the speaker is able to select one particular sentence out of all possible permissible sentences, even though the question of *why* a particular sentence is selected may be due to non-linguistic motivational factors. Even thus restricted to the problem of *how* the speaker selects his options, this requirement can be subdivided into two aspects: how the speaker chooses the *content* of 'what he wants to say' and how he selects an appropriate *form* for expressing this content.

Considering Chomsky's theory first, it was precisely in order to fulfil the aim of devising a set of formal rules that would generate only correct sentences that transformational rules were developed. Chomsky demonstrated that a system confined to phrase structure rules, in which individual symbols are rewritten independently, would result in an extremely cumbersome and unrevealing statement of the structural relations that have to be taken into account when generating sentences. Transformational rules, which operate on the overall structure of a string, make it possible to express interdependence relations governing the generation of different parts of a sentence; thus allowing many necessary grammatical rules to be formulated, such as agreement of number and gender, correct selection of pronouns, choice of transitive and intransitive verbs in appropriate frameworks, correct ordering of words in questions and passives, to mention just a few among innumerable examples. In the absence of such rules the grammar would inevitably generate many incorrect strings.

Turning to Yngve's model, which relies solely on phrase structure rewriting rules, there can be no doubt that it is far less well worked out in this respect; being limited in the number of sentence types it can produce, and producing many anomalous strings. On the first weaker criterion, then, of formulating a set of rules for producing all sentences and no non-sentences, a transformational grammar of the kind proposed by Chomsky provides a better approximation to the output of a native speaker.

Coming to the stronger requirement that a speech production model should be able to explain the speaker's ability to produce particular sentences, it would at first seem that Yngve's model has the advantage that it was specifically designed to represent the operations by which a speaker might go about producing a sentence. The program of rewriting rules is planned to output the succeeding words in a sentence in order as they occur from left to right, later units in the sentence being stored until they are finally decoded. The idea behind this is that, while the speaker has minimum commitments to finish a sentence grammatically, the rewriting of high level units into actual words is not necessarily foreseen until the speaker arrives at that point in the sentence. This tries to get round the implausible notion that a complete grammatical framework has to be generated before any words can be produced.

In contrast, Chomsky's line has been to ignore the whole problem on the grounds that it is not the function of a grammatical theory of linguistic competence to provide a model of the processes involved in speech production and perception. Leaving aside for the moment the compatibility of this position with Chomsky's other claims for linguistic competence, the interesting thing is that a transformational model of the Chomskyan type provides a more feasible basis for the ability to produce speech than the superficially more plausible Yngve model with its concentration on left-to-right production of words.

A major problem with Yngve's model is that, since each branch of the sentence is rewritten independently, there is no point at which either the content or the form of a sentence can be centrally planned. As the left-to-right production of a sentence proceeds, predicate, NP, VP, N and other symbols are taken out of storage and rewritten at random, regardless of what the prior words in the sentence have been. It is difficult to see how allowance could be made for initial choice of semantic content, or what the speaker 'wants to say'. Further, given that semantic content has in some way already been selected, how would it even be possible to select rewriting rules so as to minimize memory storage commitments? Yngve suggests that a machine subject to human memory limitations might incorporate an 'alarm' cut off point when depth approaches more than 7, i.e. seven symbols having to be stored at once. This presumably means that a speaker would start producing a sentence at random but suddenly have to break off if the limit of manageable depth is overstepped. Yngve's other proposal is that the grammatical rules themselves contain restrictions to prevent overloading of memory storage; while more plausible, this remains to be worked out in formal terms. The essential point is that, without building in knowledge of overall structure, there is no easy way of taking such considerations into account when selecting the individual words of a sentence.

With a two-level theory such as Chomsky's, however, it seems a reasonable assumption that a speaker first generates a deep structure containing a series of interlinked 'kernel' propositions representing the semantic content of 'what he wants to say'. Choice of alternative surface forms would be a matter of attaching appropriate tags to the deep structure indicating which transformations should come into force. It is true that the process of generating deep structure by phrase structure rules comes up against the same problem as Yngve's model in that the random generation of individual symbols independently would make it impossible for an initial overall semantic content to be selected. Indeed, Chomsky's grammar goes even further than Yngve's in requiring that a complete deep structure framework must be generated prior to the insertion of actual words, since without information about the overall structure of a sentence it would be impossible to formulate rules for the correct selection of words from the lexicon.

Undoubtedly, the notion that a speaker goes about expressing 'what he wants to say' by first generating an abstract NP, VP syntactic structure and only then choosing words has always seemed inherently implausible. What might be claimed, however, is that the distinction between deep and surface structure made in transformational grammar has led to recognition of a new and possibly more manageable problem:

assuming that the *content* of a response is already given, what factors determine the *form* in which it is expressed? Deciding among all the various alternatives for expressing an 'idea' is a complex enough task, even when isolated from the need to explain how that particular semantic content was selected in the first place. Many of the experiments on semantic function described on pages 116ff come within this rubric. The semantic content of a sentence is assumed to be given and the interest lies in investigating the contexts in which its expression in negative, passive or other syntactic form is most appropriate. While it is obvious that the context in which an utterance is made affects choice of semantic content as well as the form in which it is expressed, separation of these two aspects has opened up new ways of looking at the operations involved in sentence production.

Touching on just this point, an illuminating comparison between Chomsky's transformational theory and Yngve's surface structure model can be found in their treatment of the topic of language translation, since in this case choice of semantic content has already been made in the first language. Yngve's model was originally designed as a machine translation program for generating an equivalent sentence in a second language. The basic idea was that each word in the first language sentence would be looked up in some sort of dictionary which would have to provide not only the appropriate word in the second language but also an indication of the role that the word is playing in the sentence as a whole. Given these facts, the program in Yngve's model was designed to generate a correct sentence with the same meaning in the second language.

However, in spite of early optimism, Yngve admitted in a second report to the American Philosophical Society in 1964 that, although the language generating program had led to many insights into the grammatical structure of English and other languages, the use of it for translation from one language to another had come up against what he called the 'semantic barrier'. Among attempts to get round this he describes research being carried out on the problem of extracting logical relations from the structures of sentences, such as implication in *If so and so, then such and such* type of sentences. This does indeed seem to represent a major retreat from relying solely on surface structure analysis.

At this point it is of interest to compare the implications of Chomsky's theory for prospects of machine translation. It has been suggested that the translation process should take place at the deep structure level for two main reasons. First, it is the deep structure that contains the information necessary for semantic interpretation, including not only the possible meanings of the words but also underlying relations between logical subject and object, and so on. Even more relevant for this purpose is the argument that deep structure relations are universal across languages. If this is the case, then all that would be required is to reduce a sentence in the first language to its deep structure, make an automatic transfer by means of linguistic universals to an equivalent deep structure in the second language, and finally generate an appropriate surface structure. This would appear to avoid all the difficulties attributable to the many surface form variations in different languages by carrying out the analysis at a level where the rules of universal grammar apply. Equally, a good case could be made for basing second language teaching on the same principles. If the learner was encouraged to acquire the deep structure of a foreign language, not only would this have much in common with his knowledge of the deep structure of his own language; but he would also learn the foreign language transformations for turning deep structures into surface structures, rather than attempting to learn unsystematic connections between the surface structures of the two languages.

Plausible as this may sound, it must be admitted that a workable method of machine translation based on universality of deep structures has not as yet been developed, or at any rate only in a form that requires a great deal of human cooperation to arrive at a translation acceptable to a native speaker. Clearly, deep structure analysis as so far carried out has not managed to transcend inter-language differences in expressing semantic 'ideas'.

It is this sort of argument that has led psychologists to take an interest in alternative linguistic formulations such as Fillmore's case grammar and generative semantics (see page 83ff). The proposal is that an 'idea' takes the form of a cluster of interrelated semantic features specifying who does what to whom with what. Thus, it is more likely that a speaker will be thinking in terms of a transaction involving a car changing hands between two males commonly known as Harry and John rather than being committed to a particular deep structure configuration such as *John bought the car from Harry*. Evidence has been quoted showing that subjects confuse in their memory a sentence like *John liked the painting and bought it from the duchess* with other sentences such as *The painting pleased John and the duchess sold it to him*, which have different deep structures but similar semantic representations (Johnson-Laird and Stevenson, 1970). This has been interpreted as evidence that the level at which people process semantic content is even more abstract than a particular deep structure configuration.

It might seem to follow from the foregoing discussion that what is required is neither a *one-level* theory, concentrating only on surface structure, nor a *two-level* deep and surface structure theory, but rather a *three-level* model incorporating semantic representation of 'ideas', deep structure syntactic relations and surface structure final ordering of words. Alternatively, it has been suggested (Johnson-Laird, 1970) that psychologically the deep structure level has no independent status because its analysis can be fully accounted for in terms of surface structure cues and knowledge of the structural properties of word meanings.

But it is just this point that is at issue between Chomsky and the generative semanticists (see discussion on page 85ff). As argued there, if it is merely a matter of defining deep structure as the level of analysis which contains all the information necessary for semantic interpretation, then the obvious answer is to extend it to include all semantic distinctions. One implication is that lexical semantic features inserted in deep structure would have to include reciprocal relationships between *buy* and *sell*, *like* and *pleased by*, *present* and *absent*, and so on.

Further support for this position is provided by Clark's (1970, 1971) work on what he calls inherent negatives, such as *John is absent*. In the course of a series of experiments testing his information processing model of negation (see page 121ff), Clark showed that subjects asked to evaluate the truth value of sentences like *The star is absent* gave patterns of reaction times similar to those obtained with explicit negatives like *The star isn't present* rather than patterns associated with the affirmatives like *The star is present*. From this he argues that semantic representation of *The star is absent* must include the negative concept of (*false* (*present*)), indicating the relationship between present and absent.

Largely due to such subtle explorations of subjects' understanding of semantic content, the problem of the proper relationship between semantic representation and deep structure is at present far from solution. For one thing, it is not clear whether deep structure can be extended to include semantic distinctions while retaining its original linguistic insights. For another, Chomsky himself, as described on pp. 86–8, has complicated the issue by introducing the notion that surface structure may also be involved in certain aspects of meaning. Finally, even if it can be demonstrated that semantic representation is an independent level of analysis, there still remains the difficulty that such an analysis merely pushes choice of options back to an earlier stage. Just as at some point it is necessary to select a passive or negative transformation marker to arrive at a particular surface structure, so options about alternative forms of a semantic 'idea' would have to be taken up. Thus, in the above example of John buying a car from Harry, a complex series of selection rules would be required to ensure that, once *Harry* had been chosen as the subject, the verb *sold* would have to be selected in order to preserve the correct meaning relationships. Equally, if *the car* was chosen as subject, the sentence would have to be recast in the passive.

The problem is that our knowledge of what occurs at most stages of sentence production is negligible. To start at the beginning, one would have to be able to explain why a semantic 'idea' should be stimulated in a particular context. Next, how does the speaker select a correct combination of syntactic structure and individual words, taking into account both deep structure relations between his 'ideas' and a surface form appropriate to the context? Assuming that his semantic 'idea' is some sort of abstract representation, which can be expressed by many alternative choices of syntactic frame and lexical items, how does the speaker select a left-to-right sequence of words, at the same time maintaining an overall grammatical structure that preserves his original meaning?

Mention should be made in this connection of an attempt by Osgood (1963) to reconcile the new psycholinguistic emphasis on generative rules with a stimulus-response approach to the left-to-right probabilities of particular words being selected. As shown in Figure 18, the idea is that the vertical bi-directional arrows represent encoding and decoding operations, while the horizontal clusters of arrows represent sets of transitional probabilities operating at every level of linguistic structure. Thus, at the topmost level there is a set of probabilities that this particular sentence has followed and will be followed by other sentences; at the next level there is a high probability that a NP will be followed by a VP; at the next an article has varying probabilities of being followed by a noun or an adjective; while at the lowest level words have different probabilities of being followed by other words, subject presumably to semantic and contextual contingencies.

The attraction of this model is that it gives expression to the indisputable fact that some left-to-right sequences of words are more probable than others. To take an extreme example, after the word *green*, *pastures* is a more probable word than *ideas*, except in the rarified atmosphere of linguistic examples (*colourless green ideas* etc.). To prove the point, one only has to think of the difference between producing a predictable cliché and an original expression. From the listener's point of view, too, it has been repeatedly shown that the more predictable an utterance the easier it is to deal with.

Unfortunately, appealing as is Osgood's attempted reconciliation, it is a statement of the problem rather than a solution.

For one thing, there is the difficulty that with a recursive system of rules allowing an infinite number of sentence structures there is in principle no way of calculating the probabilities of a particular unit following another at any particular level. Secondly, not all constraints on selection of units and words operate in a left-to-right fashion depending only on

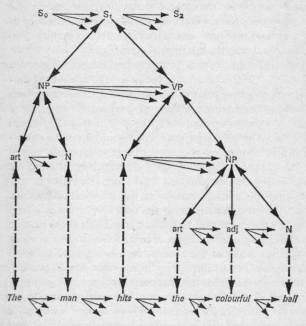

Figure 18 (From Osgood, 1963)

what has gone before. For instance, in a sentence such as *As she was feeling ill, Lucy missed the party*, the choice of pronoun is determined by the gender of the main clause subject which comes later in the sentence. A third point is that, although Osgood emphasizes the necessity for choice of semantic content preceding choice of syntactic form, in effect the top-to-bottom structure proposed in Figure 18 implies that choice of higher level syntactic units is a prerequisite for calculating the probabilities of particular words following each other. In a later article Osgood (1968) attempts to circumvent this problem by proposing a model which generates semantic deep structures, although he acknowledges the difficulties involved in explaining how the speaker gets from these to acceptable left-to-right surface structures.

Finally, there is the crucial point that, even given that probabilities can be calculated, they are not themselves the *cause* of language behaviour but rather the *result* of all kinds of syntactic, semantic, phonological and contextual rules. The task of the psychologist is to unravel the interacting variables that result in one word being more likely to occur than another in a particular context. The rationale behind psycholinguistic thinking is that an essential factor governing the probabilities of language behaviour is the speaker's knowledge (not necessarily conscious) of his language. Without taking into account grammatical constraints and syntactic rules for relating meaning and form, no progress can be made in predicting a language user's verbal behaviour; nor any insight gained into how these linguistic factors interact with cognitive and perceptual abilities, motivational states and contextual situation.

But when it comes to charting the role of grammatical analysis in accounting for the language user's behaviour, the many difficulties involved are typified by an interesting suggestion recently put forward by Bever (1971). This is that the ability of linguists to construct transformational grammars which are in accordance with the intuitions of sophisticated native speakers is itself an example of language behaviour at its highest level of development. But, he goes on to propose, in the context of carrying out different tasks and certainly at different stages of development, we are not always aware of such subtle linguistic relationships. More crucially, he claims that subjects' performance on certain linguistic tasks show that they are responding on the basis of cruder or less generally significant relationships. He gives as an example an experiment with actives, passives and pseudo-passives such as *The dogs were interested in the cat*. Subjects' immediate recall performance was in line with a derivation of such sentences which does not reflect the greatest possible number of significant linguistic generalizations. On the other hand, when subjects were asked to recall the sentences after an hour, or were exposed to a wider range of similar sentences, their performance fitted in better with a more sophisticated linguistic analysis.

Bever argues that, in their attempt to devise rules that account for an increasing number of syntactic constructions, linguists find themselves forced to adopt more abstract and complex underlying generalizations. In just the same way, subjects, according to the task and their degree of experience, can show in their behaviour more or less abstract regularities, regardless of whether they are aware of them or not. This line of thought leads Bever to propose that the performance of the speaker and hearer can be characterized not just by one fully developed grammar of a language but by one of several grammars depending on the circumstances and the stage of an individual's linguistic development. The idea that, not only may different speakers have somewhat different grammars, but that the linguistic competence of a particular speaker may vary from time to time certainly throws a spanner in the work of discovering *a* grammatical model to represent the language user's abilities.

However, although this may appear to be a pessimistic conclusion concerning the validity of transformational grammar as a basis for models of language use, it is nevertheless clear that awareness of these problems and empirical research directed to their solution were directly stimulated by the revolutionary approach to language embodied in Chomsky's theory. An attempt will be made to arrive at a final balance sheet of profits and losses in the concluding chapter.

Summary

Models of language use can be based either on deep and surface structure or on surface structure only. Deep structure models can be further subdivided according to whether the operations for mapping deep on to surface structure are transformational or take some other form.

Transformational deep structure models

These (e.g. Katz and Postal, 1964) come up against both the theoretical implausibility of people using transformational rules in the order and form specified by transformational grammar and empirical evidence that subjects do not carry out syntactic, phonological and semantic analyses independently of each other.

Non-transformational deep structure models

These (e.g. Fodor and Garrett, 1967, Fodor, Garrett and Bever, 1968) propose that people use perceptual mapping operations utilizing a mixture of phonological, lexical, semantic and syntactic cues to extract deep structure relations from surface structure. This implies that analysis begins as soon as the words of a sentence start unfolding from left to right.

Surface structure models

These (e.g. Yngve, 1960, 1962, 1964, Johnson, 1965, 1966a, b, 1969) claim that sentence production, perception and recall can be accounted for solely in terms of phrase structure analysis of the final left-to-right surface order of words in a sentence. Experiments (Martin and Roberts, 1966, 1967, Martin, Roberts and Collins, 1968, Wright, 1969, Perfetti, 1969) demonstrated the difficulties of handling semantic factors within a surface structure framework. Other work (Fodor and Bever, 1965, Bever, 1971, Levelt, 1970) showed that deep structure has to be taken into account in explaining subjects' sentence processing performance.

Concluding points

On both theoretical and experimental grounds it appears that the two-level concepts of deep and surface structure have psychological reality, although the operations for extracting 'meaningful' deep structure from surface structure word order need not take the form of transformational rules. It is also argued that some form of deep structure representation is necessary to account for a speaker's ability to express 'meanings' in sentence form. There is, however, much controversy as to whether underlying deep structure should be formulated as specified in transformational grammar or in the form of an even more abstract semantic representation.

7 The Final Reckoning: Before and After

Perhaps the fairest way to evaluate the overall impact of the psycholinguistic approach is to compare the study of language before and after the Chomskyan revolution. As indicated in the introduction, the major emphasis had been on treating language as a series of verbal responses, or in the more complex mediation theories of Osgood and others, as mediated by conditioned responses representing the meanings of words. The question of how words are combined in utterances was looked at either as some form of generalization from combinations already experienced, as in Skinner's account, or analysed in information theory terms as being dependent on the probabilities of particular words occurring in a particular sequence.

A major effect of Chomsky's generative linguistics was to bring to psychologists' attention the crucial importance of linguistic creativity. By demonstrating that the competence of a language user includes the ability to produce a potentially infinite number of possible sentences, Chomsky made psychologists aware that language is a far more complicated kind of behaviour than had hitherto been appreciated. Far from helping psychologists to *solve* the language problem, the initial, and indeed continuing, effect of attempts to write fully adequate generative grammars has been to induce a healthy respect for the complexities of language behaviour, thereby cutting off some attractive avenues of over-simplification.

Apart from the introduction of generative principles, what has been the contribution of the particular formulation of transformational grammar proposed by Chomsky? The first point is that raised earlier concerning different interpretations of linguistic competence. According to the weaker, or more neutral, definition, transformational grammar makes available a description of the structure of linguistic usage. The search for the 'best' set of grammatical rules for describing language has been governed by Chomsky's concepts of linguistic criteria. Not only must a grammar have the weak generative capacity of being able to generate all possible sentences in a language (observational adequacy) but it must also have the strong generative capacity of being able to match a native speaker's intuitions about semantic relations and distinctions (descriptive adequacy). Finally, the rules must achieve the most economical description of a language on the basis of linguistic universals which specify underlying regularities common to all languages (explanatory adequacy).

On the basis of all three criteria, Chomsky was able to show that linguistic usage can only be fully explained by a two-level theory, expressed as 'kernels' and transformations in the 1957 theory and deep and surface structure in the 1965 theory. Through this clarification of the native speaker's usage, Chomsky's theory in its turn provides a criterion which any psychological model of the language user will have to match.

But, as was argued in the section on competence and performance, it is easy to slip from a description of the regularities observed in linguistic usage into the stronger claim that grammatical analysis describes the internalized knowledge upon which the speaker draws when producing and understanding sentences. The value of this hypothesis is that it has led to a great deal of research into what is actually happening in language behaviour. The most reasonable conclusion at present would appear to be that sentence processing, and any plausible model of speech production, involves at least two levels of analysis, deep structure and surface structure. However, the operations used to relate one level to the other have less to do with transformational operations than with utilization of direct perceptual mapping rules based on a variety of interacting syntactic, semantic and phonological cues.

The most important feature of this two-level approach is its emphasis on the relation between underlying semantic content and syntactic form. Paradoxical as it may seem, Chomsky's initial insistence on the independence of syntax from semantics has led to a more far-reaching appreciation of the complexity of the interaction between the two. The only purpose of syntactic rules is to express semantic relationships, the meaning of sentences being determined by the syntactic relations holding between individual words. Thus, to know how to speak a foreign language it is not sufficient to know the meanings of every word in its vocabulary, unless one also knows the rules for combining these to produce meaningful sentences. By his formalization of the relationship between the syntactic and semantic components in the 1965 theory, Chomsky made it possible to conceptualize the interaction between syntax and semantics in terms of the listener extracting the deep structure relations necessary for semantic interpretation from the surface order of words in a sentence. This in turn has opened up the question of whether deep structure itself contains all the information necessary for expressing semantic distinctions and similarities; or whether a third level of semantic representation is required. At present three alternatives are still the subject of much discussion:

1. adding an additional level of semantic representation;
2. replacing deep structure by semantic representation;
3. extending deep structure analysis to include necessary semantic relationships.

What the whole argument undoubtedly demonstrates is increased awareness of the complex processes involved in speakers' understanding of semantic content.

Looking at the same problem from the speech production side has drawn attention to the extreme difficulty of specifying how a speaker is able to choose an appropriate combination of syntactic frame and individual words to express his meaning. In general, the whole question of the speaker's options for selecting a particular left-to-right sequence of words has proved difficult to handle within a generative grammar containing random rewriting rules.

The attempt to develop a model of speech production raises again the issue of what should be the proper relationship between the disciplines of linguistics and psychology. According to the weaker definition of competence there is no overlap, since linguistic descriptions are only concerned with *what* knowledge of a language consists of. But, as a result of taking up the stronger claim that grammatical rules are internalized in the speaker, both psychologists and linguists are interested in describing *how* someone who knows a language is able to produce utterances that are accepted as meaningful by other native speakers. However, there are still other questions the psychologist would like to ask: first, given an adequate description of the language user's ability to produce sentences, *why* is this ability used to produce particular utterances on particular occasions; secondly, how does a child *acquire* this ability in the first place.

On the first of these questions, Chomsky (1966b, p. 55 in Lester, 1970) states that linguistic behaviour is 'stimulus-free and innovative'. Because repetition of fixed phrases is a rarity, 'it is only under exceptional and quite uninteresting circumstances that one can seriously consider how "situational context" determines what is said, even in probabilistic terms'. This position is clearly in direct opposition to Skinner's claim that all verbal behaviour is under stimulus control. What this great controversy comes down to is that each of the protagonists is looking at only one aspect of language. Both the theoretical arguments and experimental evidence quoted in this book go to show that people's ability to use language cannot be explained in terms of generalization of stimulus-response associations. Just to take one point, analysis of the surface order of words as they occur in overt verbal responses has been demonstrated to be an inadequate explanation of how people produce and understand sentences.

On the other hand, as has been pointed out by MacCorquodale (1970) in a valiant defence of Skinner, Chomsky leaves the competent speaker with nothing to say. As long as the *what* of a verbal response is not reduced to a Skinnerian 'ouch' to the prick of a pin, it makes perfect sense to ask under what stimulus conditions a speaker will make use of his knowledge of complex linguistic rules to produce a particular utterance. Otherwise, when Chomsky says that language behaviour is undetermined even probabilistically, does he mean that it is never true to say that some utterances are more likely than others in a particular context? The failure of the Chomskyan and Skinnerian approaches to interact in meaningful discussion is because Chomsky sees no problem here while Skinner thinks he has already solved it.

To state the obvious fact that utterances vary in predictability may seem to be ignoring the point that most utterances are novel; in which case there are no prior probabilities on which predictions can be based. The crucial difference is that with probabilistic models, the attempt is made to calculate *future* probabilities of word sequences on the basis of *prior* frequencies of occurrence. From this the implication follows that the speaker proceeds through a sentence by calculating these prior probabilities; while the listener, too, bases his expectancies on his experience of these same prior frequencies. The claim being put forward here is the very different one that it may be possible to predict a speaker's choice of utterance taking into account both his knowledge of linguistic rules and relevant information about his internal state and external situation. On this basis there is no reason why the predicted utterance should not be completely novel, the focus of investigation being the circumstances under which the speaker will use his ability to produce novel sentences in a certain way. It may, indeed, prove so difficult to disentangle all the variables affecting language use that it looks as if any one utterance is unpredictable in terms of antecedent and present conditions; but to accept this would mean abandoning the hope of providing a scientific explanation of the causes of language behaviour.

One recent attempt to do just this has been described by Osgood (1971). His technique was to try and predict both the content and form of the sentences people would choose to describe simple situations (such as a man holding a blue ball, a black ball rolling and hitting a blue ball, a ball hitting or missing a tube, and so on) to an imaginary listener. The idea was that by manipulating the sequence of events one could influence the probability that subjects would refer to certain aspects of the situations and express the relations between these in a certain way. Examples were the frequent use of adjectives to identify an object at its first appearance or to distinguish it from similar objects; the tendency as objects became more familiar through repeated presentation to drop out adjectives, use *the ball* instead of *a ball* and to use pronouns instead of nouns; systematic choice of tense to describe completed or contemporaneous events; use of *and* or *but* to describe common or antagonistic actions; and finally choice of negatives to express unfulfilled expectations.

This approach is an extension of the idea behind the experiments on the semantic function of negatives and passives (described on p. 116ff), since it aims to discover the conditions in which it is natural to use a wide range of linguistic constructions. Osgood goes on to claim that generative grammar is incapable of accounting for speakers' ability to use language in this way because the situational conditions to which they are responding are perceptual and cognitive rather than linguistic. As Osgood points out, the subject's choice of utterance is based on awareness of shared presuppositions between speaker and listener about the objective context; for instance, that a blue ball has already been presented or that one might expect to find something on the table.

An interesting point is that what was earlier introduced as an attempt to get at *why* people should produce particular utterances in certain situations, has already shifted back to the question of *how* a speaker is able to use language in this way. One might still like to keep a distinction between the language user's ability to select sentences and the circumstances in which he chooses to do so. But the difficulty of drawing this line between linguistic and psychological concerns is demonstrated by a quotation from a recent article by Chomsky (1971). When discussing the need for surface structure stress to be taken into account in order to determine presuppositions about possible responses to an utterance, Chomsky writes (p. 205): 'The notions "focus", "presupposition", and "shared presupposition" (even in cases where the presupposition may not be expressible by a grammatical sentence) must be determinable from the semantic interpretation of sentences, if we are to be able to explain how discourse is constructed and, in general, how language is used.' Of course, Chomsky is concerned only with linguistic evidence provided by analysis of the sentence itself. But with such an extension of competence to cover awareness of presuppositions, one is getting near to a definition of competence that has been recently proposed by Campbell and Wales (1970, p. 247) as 'the ability to produce or understand utterances which are not so much *grammatical* but, more important, *appropriate to the context in which they are made*' (authors' italics). This implies that a model of the language user will have to cover not only the speaker's ability to produce all permissible sentences, and the operations by which a particular sentence can be selected, but also his ability to make that selection taking into account his own and his listener's awareness of the context; (even when this may not be the immediate physical environment but rather a shared internal reference to some abstract realm of discourse).

Some of the same arguments apply to the child's acquisition of language, a subject which has hardly been touched upon in this book. Transformational linguists have provided an account of *what* a child learns, based on the assumption that the child is gradually internalizing the full grammar of adult language; and backed up by analyses of child grammars which provide plenty of evidence that learning cannot be explained as reinforced imitation of stimulus-response associations (for a stimulating account of this approach see McNeill, 1970). On the other hand, it is not enough to say with Chomsky that the child must have an innate linguistic ability which enables it to discover just those transformational rules that will generate the sentences in a language most economically. Given the human predisposition to learn human languages, apparently lacking in animals, what is needed is an account of the learning mechanisms by which a child arrives at the rules of the particular language to which he is exposed. As long as allowance is made for the complexity of *what* is learnt, there is no reason why psychologists should not try out various learning theories to explain *how* it is learnt. Once again the function of linguistic description is to prevent over-simplification of the behaviour being studied.

When trying to sum up the contribution of transformational grammar to psychology, one point that must be stressed is that the psycholinguistic approach has opened up totally new ways of conceptualizing language. The experiments described in this book, which it is fair to say would never have been carried out except under the stimulus of transformational grammar, are a far cry from *simpliste* pre-Chomskyan attempts to look at verbal associations and so on. By directing attention to subjects' behaviour when using sentences, the search for an exact one-to-one relationship between grammatical rules and subjects' performance has by its very failure brought to light the influence of many unexpected factors.

Faced with this sort of experimental evidence about subjects' language use, it is, of course, perfectly logical for Chomsky to fall back on the position that it is a misunderstanding of generative grammar to treat it as a model for the production and perception of sentences. It is a fair point, too, that for purposes of grammatical analysis it is necessary to concentrate on standard usage, ignoring moment to moment fluctuations in individual utterances. But when Chomsky makes the stronger claim that he is describing the structure of cognitive processes, can he ignore the extreme complexity of the relation between speakers' linguistic knowledge and how it is actually put to use in the real world? It would be a pity if the previous blindness of psychologists were to be matched by an equal reluctance on the part of transformational linguists to face up to facts about language use that do not square with their account of the organization of linguistic rules. When one looks at all that remains to be discovered about the learning and use of man's most important faculty, one hopes that, rather than succumbing to disenchantment or taking up embattled positions from which they point out only the weaknesses of their opponents' theories, psychologists and linguists will meet the challenge of trying to find a theory that will account for all aspects of language.

References

ALLEN, J. P. B., and VAN BUREN, P. (1971), *Chomsky: Selected Readings*, Oxford University Press.

BEVER, T. G. (1970), 'The influence of speech performance on linguistic structures', in G. B. Flores d'Arcais and W. J. M. Levelt, (eds.), *Advances in Psycholinguistics*, North-Holland.

BEVER, T. G. (1971), 'The integrated study of language behaviour', in J. Morton, (ed.), *Biological and Social Factors in Psycholinguistics*, Logos.

BOLINGER, D. L. (1965), 'The atomization of meaning', *Language*, vol. 41, pp. 555–73. (Reprinted in Jakobovits and Miron, 1967.)

BROADBENT, D. E. (1970), 'In defence of empirical psychology', *Bull. Brit. Psychol. Soc.*, vol. 23, pp. 87–96.

CAMPBELL, R. and WALES, R. (1970), 'The study of language acquisition', in J. Lyons, (ed.), *New Horizons in Linguistics*, Penguin.

CHASE, W. G. and CLARK, H. H. (1972) 'Mental operations in the comparison of sentences and pictures', in L. Gregg, (ed.), *Cognition in Learning and Memory*, Wiley.

CHOMSKY, N. (1957), *Syntactic Structures*, Mouton.

CHOMSKY, N. (1959), Review of *Verbal Behaviour* by B. F. Skinner, *Language*, vol. 35, pp. 26–58. (Reprinted in Jakobovits and Miron, 1967.)

CHOMSKY, N. (1964), Formal discussion of 'The development of grammar in child language' by W. Miller and S. Ervin, in U. Bellugi and R. Brown, (eds.), *The Acquisition of Language* (Monographs of Soc. for Research in Child Dev., 92), Child Development Publications. (Reprinted in Lester, 1970.)

CHOMSKY, N. (1965), *Aspects of the Theory of Syntax*, Mouton.

CHOMSKY, N. (1966a), *Topics in the Theory of Generative Grammar*, Mouton.

CHOMSKY, N. (1966b), 'Linguistic theory', in R. G. Mead, Jr., (ed.), *Language Teaching: Broader Contexts*, Northeast Conference Reports. (Reprinted in Lester, 1970; also in Allen and Van Buren, 1971.)

CHOMSKY, N. (1968), *Language and Mind*, Harcourt, Brace and World.

CHOMSKY, N. (1970), 'Remarks on nominalisation', in R. A. Jacobs and P. S. Rosenbaum, (eds.), *Readings in English Transformational Grammar*, Ginn and Company.

CHOMSKY, N. (1971), 'Deep structure, surface structure, and semantic interpretation', in D. D. Steinberg and L. A. Jakobovits, (eds.), *Semantics: An Interdisciplinary Reader in Philosophy, Linguistics and Psychology*, Cambridge University Press.

CHOMSKY, N. (1972), *Problems of Knowledge and Freedom*, Fontana.

CHOMSKY, N. and HALLE, M. (1968), *The Sound Pattern of English*, Harper and Row.

CLARK, H. H. (1965), 'Some structural properties of simple active and passive sentences', *J. Verb. Learn. Verb. Behav.*, vol. 4, pp. 365–70.

CLARK, H. H. (1970), 'How we understand negation', Paper presented at COBRE Workshop on Cognitive Organization and Psychological Processes, Huntingdon Beach, California.

CLARK, H. H. (1971), 'The chronometric study of meaning components,' Paper presented at C.R.N.S. Colloque International sur les Problèmes Actuels de Psycholinguistique, Paris.

CLARK, H. H. (in press), 'Semantics and comprehension', in T. A. Sebeok (ed.), *Current Trends in Linguistics*, vol. 12: *Linguistics and Adjacent Arts and Sciences*, Mouton.

CLARK, H. H. and CHASE, W. G. (in press), 'On the process of comparing sentences against pictures', *Cognitive Psychology*.

FILLMORE, C. J. (1968), 'The case for case', in E. Bach and R. T. Harms, (eds.), *Universals in Linguistic Theory*, Holt, Rinehart and Winston.

FODOR, J. A. and BEVER, T. G. (1965), 'The psychological reality of linguistic segments', *J. Verb. Learn. Verb. Behav.*, vol. 4, pp. 414–20. (Reprinted in Jakobovits and Miron, 1967.)

FODOR, J. A. and GARRETT, M. (1967), 'Some syntactic determinants of sentential complexity', *Perception and Psychophysics*, vol. 2, pp. 289–96.

FODOR, J. A., GARRETT, M. and BEVER, T. G. (1968), 'Some syntactic determinants of sentential complexity, 11: verb structure', *Perception and Psychophysics*, vol. 3, pp. 453–61.

GOUGH, P. B. (1965), 'Grammatical transformations and speed of understanding', *J. Verb. Learn. Verb. Behav.*, vol. 4, pp. 107–11.

GOUGH, P. B. (1966), 'The verification of sentences: the effects of delay of evidence and sentence length', *J. Verb. Learn. Verb. Behav.*, vol. 5, pp. 492–6.

GREENBAUM, S. and QUIRK, R. (1970), *Elicitation Experiments in English: Linguistic Studies in Use and Attitude*, Longman.

GREENE, J. M. (1970a), 'The semantic function of negatives and passives', *Brit. J. Psychol.*, vol. 61, pp. 17–22.

GREENE, J. M. (1970b), 'Syntactic form and semantic function', *Quart. J. Exp. Psychol.*, vol. 22, pp. 14–27.

HERRIOT, P. (1969), 'The comprehension of active and passive sentences as a function of pragmatic expectations', *J. Verb. Learn. Verb. Behav.*, vol. 8, pp. 166–9.

JAKOBOVITS, L. A. and MIRON, M. S. (1967), *Readings in the Psychology of Language*, Prentice-Hall.

JOHNSON, M. G. (1967), 'Syntactic position and rated meaning', *J. Verb. Learn. Verb. Behav.*, vol. 6, pp. 240–46. (Reprinted in Jakobovits and Miron, 1967.)

JOHNSON, N. F. (1965), 'The psychological reality of phrase structure rules', *J. Verb. Learn. Verb. Behav.*, vol. 4, pp. 469–75.

JOHNSON, N. F. (1966a), 'The influence of associations between elements of structured verbal responses', *J. Verb. Learn. Verb. Behav.*, vol. 5, pp. 369–74.

JOHNSON, N. F. (1966b), 'On the relationship between sentence structure and the latency in generating the sentence', *J. Verb. Learn. Verb. Behav.*, vol. 5, pp. 375–80.

JOHNSON, N. F. (1969), 'The effect of a difficult word on the transitional error probabilities within a sentence', *J. Verb. Learn. Verb. Behav.*, vol. 8, pp. 518–23.

JOHNSON, S. C. (1967), 'Heirarchical clustering schemes', *Psychometrika*, vol. 32, pp. 241–54.

JOHNSON-LAIRD, P. N. (1968), 'The choice of the passive voice in a communicative task', *Brit. J. Psychol.*, vol. 59, pp. 7–15.

JOHNSON-LAIRD, P. N. (1970), 'The perception and memory of sentences', in J. Lyons, *New Horizons in Linguistics*, Penguin.

JOHNSON-LAIRD, P. N. and STEVENSON, R. (1970), 'Memory for syntax', *Nature*, vol. 227, p. 412.

KATZ, J. J. and FODOR, J. A. (1963), 'The structure of a semantic theory', *Language*, vol. 39, pp. 170–210. (Reprinted in Jakobovits and Miron, 1967.)

KATZ, J. J. and POSTAL, P. M. (1964), *An Integrated Theory of Linguistic Descriptions*, M.I.T. Press.

LANGFORD, P. E. (in preparation), *Memory for Sentences: with special reference to the role of linguistic factors*, unpublished Ph.D. Thesis, Liverpool University.

LESTER, M. (1970), *Readings in Applied Transformational Grammar*, Holt, Rinehart and Winston.

LEVELT, W. J. M. (1970), 'A scaling approach to the study of syntactic relations', in G. B. Flores d'Arcais and W. J. M. Levelt, (eds.), *Advances in Psycholinguistics*, North-Holland.

LYONS, J. (1970), *New Horizons in Linguistics*, Penguin.

MACCORQUODALE, K. (1970), 'On Chomsky's review of Skinner's Verbal Behaviour', *J. Exp. Analysis Behav.*, vol. 13, pp. 83–99.

MCMAHON, L. E. (1963), *Grammatical Analysis as part of Understanding a Sentence*, Unpublished doctoral dissertation, Harvard University.

MCNEILL, D. (1970), *The Acquisition of Language: The Study of Developmental Psycholinguistics*, Harper and Row.

MARTIN, E. and ROBERTS, K. H. (1966), 'Grammatical factors in sentence retention', *J. Verb. Learn. Verb. Behav.*, vol. 5, pp. 211–18.

MARTIN, E. and ROBERTS, K. H. (1967), 'Sentence length and sentence retention in the free-learning situation', *Psychon. Sci.*, vol. 8, pp. 535–6.

MARTIN, E., ROBERTS, K. H. and COLLINS, A. M. (1966), 'Short term memory for sentences', *J. Verb. Learn. Verb. Behav.*, vol. 7, pp. 560–66.

MEHLER, J. (1963), 'Some effects of grammatical transformations on the recall of English sentences', *J. Verb. Learn. Verb. Behav.*, vol. 2, pp. 346–51.

MILLER, G. A. (1951), *Language and Communication*, McGraw-Hill.

MILLER, G. A. (1956), 'The magical number seven, plus or minus two: some limits on our capacity for processing information', *Psychol. Review*, vol. 60, pp. 81–97.

MILLER, G. A. and CHOMSKY, N. (1963), 'Finitary models of language users', in R. D. Luce, R. R. Bush and E. Galanter (eds.), *Handbook of Mathematical Psychology*, Wiley.

MILLER, G. A., GALANTER, E. and PRIBRAM, K. H. (1960), *Plans and the Structure of Behavior*, Holt, Rinehart and Winston.

MILLER, G. A. and McKEAN, K. E. (1964), 'A chronometric study of some relations between sentences', *Quart. J. Exp. Psych.*, vol. 16, pp. 297–308. (Reprinted in Oldfield and Marshall, 1968.)

OLDFIELD, C. and MARSHALL, J. C. (1968), *Language*, Penguin.

OSGOOD, C. E. (1963), 'On understanding and creating sentences', *Amer. Psychol.*, vol. 18, pp. 735–51. (Reprinted in Jakobovits and Miron, 1967.)

OSGOOD, C. E. (1968), 'Toward a wedding of insufficiencies', in T. R. Dixon and D. L. Horton (eds.), *Verbal Behaviour and General Behaviour Theory*, Prentice-Hall.

OSGOOD, C. E. (1971), 'Where do sentences come from?', in D. D. Steinberg and L. A. Jakobovits, *Semantics: An Interdisciplinary Reader in Philosophy, Linguistics and Psychology*, Cambridge University Press.

OSGOOD, C. E. and SEBEOK, T. A. (eds.) (1965), *Psycholinguistics: A Survey of Theory and Research Problems*, Indiana University Press.

OSGOOD, C. E., SUCI, G. J. and TANNENBAUM, P. (1957), *The Measurement of Meaning*, University of Illinois Press.

PERFETTI, C. A. (1969), 'Lexical density and phrase structure depth as variables in sentence retention', *J. Verb. Learn. Verb. Behav.*, vol. 8, pp. 719–24.

POSTAL, P. M. (1964), 'Limitations of phrase structure grammars', in J. A. Fodor and J. J. Katz (eds.), *The Structure of Language: Readings in the Philosophy of Language*, Prentice-Hall.

SAVIN, H. B. and PERCHONOCK, E. (1965), 'Grammatical structure and the immediate recall of English sentences', *J. Verb. Learn. Verb. Behav.*, vol. 4, pp. 348–53.

SCHLESINGER, I. M. (1968), *Sentence Structure and the Reading Process*, Mouton.

SHANNON, C. E. and WEAVER, W. (1949), *The Mathematical Theory of Communication*, University of Illinois Press.

SKINNER, B. F. (1957), *Verbal Behaviour*, Appleton–Century–Crofts.

SLOBIN, D. (1966), 'Grammatical transformations and sentence comprehension in childhood and adulthood', *J. Verb. Learn. Verb. Behav.*, vol. 5, pp. 219–27.

STEINBERG, D. D. and JAKOBOVITS, L. A. (1971), *Semantics: An Interdisciplinary Reader in Philosophy, Linguistics and Psychology*, Cambridge University Press.

TRABASSO, T. (1970), 'Reasoning and the processing of negative information', Invited Address, 78th Annual Convention, American Psychological Association.

TRABASSO, T. (in press), 'Mental operations in language comprehension', in J. B. Carroll and R. Freedle, (eds.), *Language Comprehension and the Acquisition of Knowledge*, Winston.

TRABASSO, T. ROLLINS, H. and SHAUGHNESSY, E. (1971), 'Storage and verification stages in processing concepts', *Cognitive Psychology*, vol. 2, pp. 239–89.

WASON, P. C. (1961), 'Response to affirmative and negative binary statements', *Brit. J. Psychol.*, vol. 52, pp. 133–42.

WASON, P. C. (1965), 'The contexts of plausible denial', *J. Verb. Learn. Verb. Behav.*, vol. 4, pp. 7–11. (Reprinted in Oldfield and Marshall, 1968.)

WASON, P. C. (1972), 'In real life negatives are false', Logique et Analyse (in press).

WASON, P. C. and JONES, S. (1963), 'Negatives: denotation and connotation', *Brit. J. Psychol.*, vol. 54, pp. 299–307.

WRIGHT, P. (1969), 'Two studies of the depth hypothesis', *Brit. J. Psychol.*, vol. 60, pp. 63–9.

YNGVE, V. (1960), 'A model and an hypothesis for language structure', *Proceedings Amer. Philosoph. Soc.*, vol. 104, pp. 444–66.

YNGVE, V. (1962), 'Computer programs for translation', *Scientific American*, vol. 206, 6, pp. 68–76.

YNGVE, V. (1964), 'Implications of mechanical translation research', *Proceedings Amer. Philosoph. Soc.*, vol. 108, pp. 275–81.

YOUNG, R. and CHASE, W. G. (1971), 'Additive stages in the comparison of sentences and pictures', Paper presented at Midwestern Psychological Association, Chicago.

Further Reading

J. P. B. Allen and P. Van Buren, *Chomsky: Selected Readings*,
Oxford University Press. 1971.
The best introduction to Chomsky's own writings, this contains
excerpts from Chomsky's principal books and articles, reordered
so as to bring together his views on major topics, and with some
helpful editorial comment.

J. Lyons, *New Horizons in Linguistics*, Penguin. 1970.
A collection of specially written articles covering both linguistic and
psycholinguistic topics. The contributions are short and deal with
most of the latest developments.

C. Oldfield and J. C. Marshall, *Language*, Penguin. 1968.
Contains a useful selection of reprinted papers on psycholinguistic
topics, including Miller and McKean (1964) and Wason (1965).

L. A. Jakobovits and M. S. Miron, *Readings in the Psychology of
Language*, Prentice-Hall. 1967.
Includes several of the key articles necessary to an understanding
of the development of psycholinguistics, including Bolinger (1965),
Chomsky's review of Skinner (1959), Fodor and Bever (1965),
Johnson (1967), Katz and Fodor (1963) and Osgood (1963).

D. D. Steinberg and L. A. Jakobovits, *Semantics*:
An Interdisciplinary Reader in Philosophy, Linguistics and Psychology,
Cambridge University Press. 1971.
The articles are at an advanced level but include the latest
developments on the crucial question of how meaning and syntax
are related, from the point of view of both linguistics (Chomsky)
and psychological models (Osgood).

D. McNeill, *The Acquisition of Language: The Study of
Developmental Psycholinguistics*, Harper and Row. 1970.
A recent exposition applying the techniques of transformational
grammar to the study of the child's language learning.

M. Lester, *Readings in Applied Transformational Grammar*, Holt,
Rinehart and Winston. 1970.
Contains interesting accounts of attempts to apply transformational
grammar to such topics as literature and style, second language
learning, and reading; includes articles by Chomsky (1964, 1966b).

Index